Audley End

Paul Drury

CONTENTS

Tour of the House

When Walden Abbey was dissolved by Henry VIII in 1538, it was granted to his loyal supporter Sir Thomas Audley (c.1487–1544). Like many other grantees of dissolved monastic houses, he promptly converted the ranges around the cloister into a courtyard house, demolishing the east end of the church, which lay on the north side.

When his successor, Thomas Howard (1561–1626), set about replacing this initial house from about 1605, his first step was to rebuild the inner courtyard ranges, still rising directly off the monastic cloister walls, with a chapel and a council chamber extending eastwards from the east wing. The kitchens occupied a separate block to the north. By the time the house was coming to completion in about 1614, Howard had added a second, outer courtyard of lodgings, approached through an enormous walled forecourt. The result was the most ambitious house built in Jacobean England. The house that can be seen today represents only a small portion of this Jacobean building; only the hall and most of the north and south wings of the inner court survived demolition during the first half of the 18th century.

Facing page: Carved figures from the Jacobean oak screen in the great hall

Audley End in about 1614

A Forecourt
B Outer court
C Lodgings
D Hall
E Kitchens
F Inner court north wing
G Inner court south wing
H Inner court east wing

THE ENTRANCE FRONT

Viewed from the west, the front of the house comprises a relatively low hall range, clasped by the taller north and south wings (and backed by the 1762 galleries). These wings date from the initial phase of building from about 1605, although the windows were sashed in the 1820s. The first-floor windows are the tallest, indicating the location of the most important rooms: the state apartments for the king and queen, which were linked by a long gallery in the lost east wing.

The style of this first building campaign is austere classical. Changes to the house in the 18th and 19th centuries have followed this style,

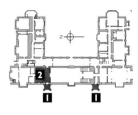

The porches, which collide rather awkwardly with the hall walls, are the main survivors of Thomas Howard's second building campaign and reflect the character of the lost outer court. Their strapwork ornament and contrasting expensive stones, superimposed on a classical architectural framework, produce an outstandingly rich effect.

2 ENTRANCE HALL (or Bucket Hall)

The north door opens into what seems to be a screens passage, in the medieval tradition, between the great hall to the right and (originally) the pantry and passage to the kitchens to the left. But the arcade on the left is Jacobean, and from the outset opened into a larger space, which would also have given direct access up the north stair to the queen's apartment in the north range. Although this was an innovation, a precursor of later entrance halls, it still functioned as the service space to the hall. The grand doorway in the wall to the left opened into a chapel created in about 1725, which rose through two storeys. An eclectic combination of furnishings was assembled here by the 3rd Lord Braybrooke (1783–1858), whose initials and coronet appear on the leather fire buckets dated 1833.

Below: View from the Bucket Hall along the (18th-century) axis beyond the great hall. The stone screen is part of Thomas Howard's second building campaign, unrelated to the framing of the floor it carries

giving it a remarkable unity. In contrast, Henry Winstanley's engraving of 1676 (see page 44) shows that the demolished outer court, added in Thomas Howard's second campaign and complete by about 1614, had a riot of ornament derived from both Flemish and French sources, illustrating the two extremes of Jacobean taste.

1 PORCHES

Audley End is unusual in having two porches on the entrance front. They not only create architectural symmetry, but also express the parallel arrangement of the king's and queen's state apartments as they were originally arranged in the south and north wings.

As an ambitious courtier, appointed Lord Chamberlain by James I soon after his accession, Thomas Howard hoped that such palatial accommodation would encourage James and his wife, Anne of Denmark, to stay at the house on their 'progresses', which James did in 1614. The scenes in the round heads of the porch doors reflect the parallel arrangement. The partly defaced one on the king's (south) side showed Mars, the god of war, in a chariot pulled by foxes, after a 16th-century German engraving by Virgil Solis; the queen's (north) side has an allegory of the arts of peace.

Above: Margaret Audley, by Hans Eworth, 1562

Below: The great hall, looking south towards the stair

◪ GREAT HALL

The great hall was the ceremonial heart of the house. While by the early 17th century only servants normally ate in the hall, with the steward presiding, its importance was growing as the place where guests were received, visitors waited and entertainments such as masques were held. The big, central arched opening (rather than the smaller rectangular ones to either side, later blocked) in the magnificent Jacobean oak screen reflects this change of emphasis, as it was better suited for making an entry than for serving food. The screen was probably once painted in bright colours.

The volume of the hall, its roof and the oak screen remain much as Thomas Howard built them, but until the 1760s there were windows in both long walls. It owes its present ambiance to the antiquarian taste of the 3rd Lord Braybrooke. In 1825–8 he stripped the screen of its 18th-century white paint, renewed the wall panelling, and had the antiquary Henry Shaw remodel the chimney piece, incorporating neoclassical statues from Robert Adam's library (page 23) alongside old woodwork. Wood carvings and 17th-century furniture bought at auction were complemented by an eclectic collection of arms and armour. The pictures on the panelling represent owners of the house, such as the impressive portrait of Margaret Audley (1540–64), mother of Thomas Howard, by Hans Eworth. The pictures above the panelling came to Audley End on the 3rd Lord Braybrooke's marriage to Lady Jane Cornwallis in 1819.

The only furnishing to survive from the time of Sir John Griffin Griffin (1719–97), owner of the house in the late 18th century, is the white marble pedestal in the Antique style in the bay, purchased from Robert Adam in 1773.

◪ STAIR

The stair was probably designed by Nicholas Dubois in about 1725 to provide a ceremonial approach to the saloon. The best stair in the Jacobean house was clearly intended to go here, behind the dais of the hall, accessible from outside the hall via the king's porch, and leading directly to the king's apartments on the first floor. It is not certain, however, if such a stair was ever built but if so, it had gone by the late 17th century; only the ceiling is original.

The screen separating the stair from the hall is a composite design. The lower part was probably designed by the architect Sir John Vanbrugh in about 1708. The upper section was certainly created by the plasterer Joseph Rose for Sir John Griffin Griffin between 1763 and 1764.

◪ SALOON

In its present form this room epitomizes the combination of modern comfort and ancient splendour that Sir John Griffin Griffin and his successors sought to create from the remains of the Jacobean Audley End. In the Jacobean period, this room would have been the great or presence chamber – the first room in the state apartment built by Thomas Howard, 1st Earl of Suffolk, to accommodate James I. The original 17th-century ceiling panels, showing scenes of sea monsters, merfolk and ships, may be an allusion to Thomas Howard's naval career, including his role in

defeating the Armada in 1588. The frieze round the walls would have incorporated similar motifs.

The painted dedication in the corner of the room tells us that the saloon was refitted by Sir John in 1785, to commemorate his elevation to the peerage as Lord Howard de Walden in the previous year. In fact he had established the decorative framework between 1765 and 1773, when he first fitted up the room as the breakfast and morning room – breakfast was taken in the large bay.

He installed the Gothick plaster frieze and new panelling in a Jacobean style, incorporating a genuine Jacobean strapwork frieze with grinning variations on the Howard lion, rescued from his aunt Lady Portsmouth's demolition of the long gallery a decade earlier.

A fashionable Italian artist, Biagio Rebecca, painted (or adapted) the sequence of portraits incorporated in the panelling. They illustrate Sir John's descent from Thomas, Lord Audley, who first made a house of Walden Abbey in 1538, and culminate in pictures of Sir John and his mother. In 1785 the room became a saloon, with a new state apartment opening off it. It was fashionably painted white, enriched with gilding, and has not been painted since. Rebecca painted the arms of Thomas Howard on the chimney piece, flanked by portraits of Henry VIII and Elizabeth I over the doors.

Sir John's formal furnishing began to be softened from the 1820s, with the introduction of centre tables and the Axminster carpet. By 1847, Mrs Bancroft, wife of the American ambassador, noted that 'not withstanding its vast size, the sofas and tables were so disposed all over the apartment as to give it the most friendly, warm and social aspect.' This trend to informal comfort continued as the 19th century progressed. The ottoman (square sofa) is a rare survival from the 1860s or 1870s.

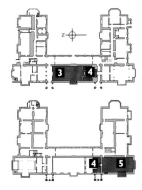

Below: The saloon looking south-eastwards, with the ottoman in the centre

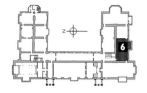

THE 19TH-CENTURY APARTMENT

This floor of the south wing was reworked as the 'new reception rooms' by the 3rd Lord Braybrooke between 1825 and 1830, following his decision to make Audley End his principal seat. In the Jacobean period, the south wing housed the king's apartment; later, in Charles II's time, it housed the queen's apartment (see plan on page 48). The upper floors at the eastern end were subsequently removed by Lady Portsmouth in 1752. It was then restored to its full height by Sir John Griffin Griffin between 1785 and 1786, after his elevation to the peerage as Lord Howard de Walden, when he created a state apartment opening off the saloon on the south side of the wing, and the 'red apartment' (so-called as it was the original location of the Red Bed) on the north.

The 3rd Lord Braybrooke used elements from the original Jacobean house and added Jacobean-style features to match, but he retained the white and gold colour scheme carried over from Sir John Griffin Griffin's saloon and state apartment. Combined with large windows, this produced exceptionally light, bright rooms.

In the early 19th century, family and guests would have assembled for dinner in the saloon, before processing to the dining room. Afterwards, they would have dispersed to the other rooms in the apartment, or returned to the saloon.

6 Drawing Room

This room is displayed as it would have appeared in the time of the 3rd Lord Braybrooke. It was his personal sitting room, and was used to display the cream of his cousin Sir John Griffin Griffin's cabinet picture collection. Works include the exquisite *Breakfast Piece* by the renowned 17th-century still-life painter Pieter Claesz and two paintings by the 17th-century Dutch landscape painter Jan van Goyen: *On the Shore at Egmond aan Zee* and *View of the Valkhof at Nijmegen*. *The Bucintoro at the Molo on Ascension Day* by Canaletto was at Audley End by 1797. The only 19th-century addition was Henry Pickersgill's 1834 portrait of Lady Braybrooke on the end wall (see page 15).

Above: Unknown Gentleman, by Hans Holbein the younger, on display in the drawing room

Right top: Watercolour of the drawing room in the 1850s with the pictures originally hung against red flock wallpaper, which has since been replaced with silk

Right: The drawing room – its chimney piece probably Jacobean work moved from the north wing

Audley End's Painting Collection

Audley End is home to an impressive collection of paintings, including Tudor and Stuart portraits, Old Masters and portrait miniatures.

The paintings now at Audley End were largely collected by Sir John Griffin Griffin in the 18th century. Sir John commissioned the sequence of dynastic portraits in the saloon from Biagio Rebecca and others, to illustrate his place in the line of succession from Thomas, Lord Audley. He acquired portraits of his Howard forbears, including Hans Eworth's compelling portrait of Margaret Audley, Duchess of Norfolk, mother of the 1st Earl of Suffolk who built the house.

Royal portraiture

Royal portraiture is, unsurprisingly, a dominant strand of the collection with almost every monarch represented from Henry VIII to George III. Sir John also acquired Italian, Dutch and Flemish Old Masters. The best of his purchases have been displayed in the drawing room since the 19th century. It was the 3rd Lord Braybrooke who arranged them in this room, adding only the portrait of his wife, Lady Jane Cornwallis, by William Henry Pickersgill.

Highlights in the drawing room include the Venetian scene of *The Bucintoro at the Molo on Ascension Day* by Canaletto (and probably other hands from his studio); Holbein's *Unknown*

Gentleman; a pair of marine landscapes from the Low Countries by van Goyen, dating from the 1640s; and Claesz's finely detailed still-life *Breakfast Piece*.

Family portraiture

Portraits of the Neville and Cornwallis families were added in the 19th century. Cornwallis portraits fill the upper register of the great hall and populate the picture gallery, whilst an imposing state portrait of the 1st Marquess Cornwallis by Sir William Beechey dominates the dining room. Late 17th-century portraiture by Peter Lely and Willem Wissing, in the fashionable and opulent style favoured by the Court at that time, are particular strengths, including Lely's superlative self-portrait with the architect Hugh May, now hanging in the north lobby.

The portrait miniatures at Audley End form a notable addition to the collection. The work of some of the best of the English and Continental miniaturists can be found here, including Nicholas Hilliard and Christian Zincke. A miniature of Louis XV after Van Loo, encrusted with diamonds and surmounted by a small crown, was a gift from the king to the father of the 2nd Lord Braybrooke.

Above: Portrait miniature of Sir Thomas Griffin by Nicholas Hilliard, 1599
Left: Pieter Claesz's Breakfast Piece, c.1640
Below: Detail from Sir Peter Lely's self-portrait with the architect Hugh May

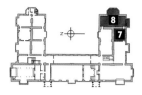

In spite of its uniform appearance, this room has been remodelled several times. It was first formed in about 1736 by amalgamating the antechamber and half the privy chamber of the queen's apartment (see plan on page 48). It was divided again by Sir John Griffin Griffin to form the anteroom and state dressing room of his state apartment, and finally reunited by the 3rd Lord Braybrooke.

No Jacobean work survived these changes, so the ceiling was recreated by the 3rd Lord Braybrooke, with a frieze based on elements from the Jacobean porches. The chimney piece was probably brought from the north wing, but its white and gold finish and the steel stove grate indicate the style of Sir John Griffin Griffin's state apartment, as does the white ground Axminster carpet of 1786–7 and the matching chairs upholstered in 1786. The

Below: A portrait of Sir John Griffin Griffin presides over the South Library

chairs are protected by 1830s-style chintz case covers. The majority of the other furniture is French, probably from the Cornwallis family collection.

7 South Library

This room is displayed as it would have looked in the early 19th century, when it was the 3rd Lord Braybrooke's private library and study. The bookcases, perhaps originally made for the 2nd Lord Braybrooke, have adjustable shelves to suit topographical works; there are also books on travel, gardening, agriculture, heraldry and genealogy. Books inherited from Sir John Griffin Griffin's library have distinctive red leather binding with a gold chequered pattern on the spine.

The Neville family's most precious relics were displayed here. The 16th-century walnut armchair that had once belonged to Alexander Pope was presented to Lord Braybrooke in 1844. The oak and walnut veneered writing table was probably made as a companion piece for it. The curtains are modern replicas of the red silk damask woven with the Neville saltire, presented by Cosimo III de' Medici, grand duke of Tuscany, to Henry Neville in 1670. The portraits of Sir John Griffin Griffin and his two wives, painted by Sir Benjamin West in 1772 (see page 53), originally in Sir John's library, and four chairs made in 1786 for the saloon, with Howard lion crests, reflected more recent historical associations.

In Charles II's time, this room formed part of the queen's bedchamber; the ceiling is in fact original (see plan on page 48). The frieze on the east wall, executed by William Wilton in 1753 when the wing was truncated, is particularly faithful to the design and spirit of the original. In 1786 Sir John Griffin Griffin made this room the state bedroom, from which the Adam chimney piece survives, reset.

8 Library

This was the 3rd Lord Braybrooke's library, created from the lady's dressing rooms of Sir John Griffin Griffin's apartments. According to Lord Braybrooke, the architects Henry Shaw and Henry Harrison 'carefully imitated [the individual elements] from examples in different parts of the house'. The ceiling was copied from the western part of the dining room, and the frieze from the south library. The pilastered panelling in the saloon inspired the bookcases made by Bennett and

'The library ... was surrounded by books in beautiful gilt bindings. In the immense bay window was a large Louis quatorze table, round which the ladies all placed themselves at their embroidery, though I preferred looking over curious illuminated missals.'
Mrs Bancroft, wife of the American ambassador, who visited Audley End in 1847

Hunt, and the frieze, executed in 1826, is an even more vigorous version of that assembled by Sir John in the saloon. The chimney piece is Jacobean, moved from the Howard bedroom in the north wing.

By the 1820s, it had become fashionable for all the family to use the library as an informal sitting room. The comfortable furnishings reflect this dual use, with a sofa flanking the fireplace and a scatter of armchairs and reading and writing tables beyond. The circular centre table, of fashionable amboyna wood, provided a focus for informal gatherings. The Brussels weave carpet is a modern reproduction of the original, as are the damask curtains. The splendid view was enhanced when the parterre garden was laid out below in 1832.

The Audley End scrapbook

In 1809 the 2nd Lord Braybrooke, Richard Aldworth Neville, created the Audley End scrapbook. Perhaps motivated by an interest in the history of the house, he collected and copied engravings and illustrations that tell the story of the house, its surroundings and its succession of residents.

The scrapbook includes plans and elevations from various stages of the building's history: from before 1600 when the converted abbey still stood, to Henry Winstanley's detailed engravings of the late 17th-century palace, and illustrations of Robert Adam's 18th-century neoclassical reception rooms for Sir John Griffin Griffin.

The scrapbook was displayed on a specially designed ebonised table. The table now stands in the library.

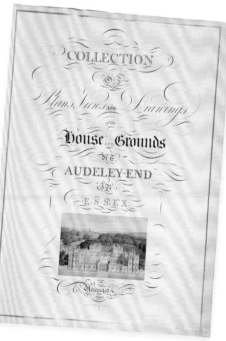

Above: The Library, created by Henry Shaw and Henry Harrison for the 3rd Lord Braybrooke
Left: The title page of the scrapbook, with a reconstruction of the Jacobean house based on Winstanley's engraving (page 42)

Right: Watercolour portrait of Joseph Romilly by a 'Miss Hervé', painted in 1836
Below: The dining room, created from two Jacobean rooms by the 3rd Lord Braybrooke in the 1820s, with Pine's portrait of George II in the background

Dining at Audley End

The clergyman and academic administrator Joseph Romilly regularly dined with the family of the 3rd Lord Braybrooke at Audley End in the 1840s and 50s. On 2 November 1846 he wrote in his diary that 'it was the first day of dining in the new dining room since its painting and gilding and new furnishing – it looked very magnificent, and the carpet and curtains are remarkably handsome'.

His diary reveals that dinners were often grand occasions with food such as turtle supplementing meat and dairy produce from the home farm and game from the estate. Exotic fruits from the garden hothouses were also on the menu: on 22 August 1847 Romilly recorded 'today some West India pine [pineapple] at dessert: I had never tasted it before: poor fruit it was'.

9 Dining Room

This was the 3rd Lord Braybrooke's dining room, redecorated in 1846, and is displayed with the table set for dessert. The mahogany sectioned dining table would have been sized to suit the number dining; spare sections would have been placed around the room as side tables. It dates from about 1810, as does one of the sideboards; the other was made to match. The modern tie-backs illustrate the original colour of the plush velvet curtains, which, with the hand-knotted Axminster carpet, added rich colour and texture to the ensemble.

As was customary in dining rooms, Lord Braybrooke hung the walls with portraits. The collection of Neville, Cornwallis and Howard relations, formed through inheritance and marriage, is dominated by Robert Pine's portrait of George II, 'universally allowed to be the most like of any in being', purchased by Sir John Griffin Griffin in 1784 and framed for his state apartment. On the opposite wall is William Beechey's portrait of the 3rd Lady Braybrooke's grandfather, the 1st Marquess Cornwallis (1738–1805), in his garter robes, flanked by her mother, Louisa (1776–1850), by Thomas Lawrence.

In the Jacobean house, this space was originally two rooms divided by a brick wall. Braybrooke's respect for surviving Jacobean decoration is clearly expressed in his retention not only of the original Jacobean ceilings but also the friezes once attached to the dividing wall. It was given some semblance of a unified interior through a matching pair of chimney pieces, one including Jacobean elements. The impressive ceiling in the western compartment

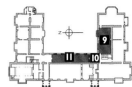

had been cut in half in about 1736 by the division of what was in Charles II's time the queen's privy chamber (plan, page 48). The roundels in the frieze represent the continents, the originals being America on the east wall and Europe on the west. The eastern part of the ceiling, once of the queen's withdrawing room, is complete.

10 SOUTH LOBBY

This provided the formal route from the saloon to the dining room; but the layout of the house meant that, extraordinarily for the early 19th century, the food had to be brought in via the same door, from the distant kitchen. The Jacobean oak stair, which led up to guest bedrooms, was altered, stripped of paint, and further embellished by Richard Neville, later 3rd Lord Braybrooke, in 1823.

The landing is hung with a set of 17th-century portraits by Sir Peter Lely, including one of Ralph, 2nd Lord Grey of Werke, whose daughter Catherine married Richard Neville of Billingbear. The pictures came to Audley End through his marriage. The miniatures are largely Griffin portraits; the finest is by Nicholas Hilliard, of Sir Thomas Griffin, dated 1599.

11 PICTURE GALLERY

This room is displayed as it appeared in the 1860s. The 4th Lord Braybrooke's natural history collection tends to dominate the 3rd Lord Braybrooke's arrangement of it as a picture gallery, between his new reception rooms in the south wing and the main family bedrooms in the north wing. It provided the setting for a dynastic display of Cornwallis family portraits, whose uniformity suggests that they had previously hung in a gallery in one of the Cornwallis ancestral homes, Brome Hall or Culford Hall, both in Suffolk. They include a 16th-century portrait of Sir Thomas Cornwallis, builder of Brome Hall, and the Hon. Henrietta Maria Cornwallis (1635–1707) by Sir Peter Lely. At the far end is a painting of Billingbear, the Neville family seat in Berkshire.

The gallery was originally added by Sir John Griffin Griffin in 1762, to connect the north and south wings at first-floor level. Its style is thoroughly Jacobean, with a strapwork ceiling by Joseph Rose, and it was perhaps inspired by the Jacobean long gallery set behind the hall at Hatfield House in Hertfordshire.

The 4th Lord Braybrooke's natural history collection, reflecting Victorian passions for natural history and collecting, accumulated here in free-standing cabinets (see page 56). In 1863 the cabinets were displaced to the newly enclosed lower gallery, and the present mounts in fitted oak cases installed. The grained woodwork, shields on

Above: Watercolour of the picture gallery in about 1850, with the free-standing cases now in the lower gallery
Below: The picture gallery today, with the fitted cases installed in 1863

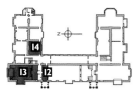

Below: Fragments of medieval stained glass from Chicksands Priory, Bedfordshire, installed here by the Ministry of Works
Bottom: The chapel in the late 18th century, with the gallery and organ visible above the tribune, and Peckitt's The Offering of the Easter Magi, *1772 (since removed) in the west window*

the cornice, cresting over the doors and the chimney piece were probably assembled at the same time, to achieve a richer, darker Jacobean ambiance. Ceramics accumulated on the cabinets, including blue and white Worcester jugs and washbowls, originally used in the state apartment. In the early 20th century, the room was fitted with a Brussels carpet and wool plush curtains (the present carpet is modern).

12 CHAPEL VESTIBULE AND 13 CHAPEL

From the time of Sir John Griffin Griffin onwards, guests and family would have assembled in the vestibule before proceeding to morning prayer in the chapel at 9.30 a.m. The vestibule was originally the gallery over the screens passage of the great hall, where musicians would have provided entertainment.

In the Jacobean house, the western corner of the first floor of the north wing housed the queen's presence chamber. A chapel was originally created here in about 1725 by removing all but the southern third of the floor of this chamber, leaving the remainder as a gallery within a two-storey chapel space. The spectacular Gothick chapel that can be seen today was created within the space of the previous chapel by joiner John Hobcraft for Sir John Griffin Griffin in about 1768. Hobcraft raised the chapel up to the first floor by reinstating the section of floor that had been removed, set a few steps below the 1725 gallery level.

Plaster and wood imitated stone, and oilcloth was used in place of a stone pavement. William Peckitt of York made painted glass windows to Biagio Rebecca's designs (the glass now in the transept window was moved here from Chicksands Priory, Bedfordshire, in the late 20th century). The specially made furniture survives as it was recorded in 1797, including the olive wood chair and the lectern by Sefferin Alkin, a fashionable 18th-century carver.

The layout reflects the social hierarchy, with the family and guests seated in a comfortable tribune (enclosed gallery) and the indoor servants in an organ gallery above it (closed in after 1826). The kitchen and outdoor staff entered by a separate stair in the north-west corner, and sat on the plain oak benches.

NORTH WING

In the Jacobean house, the north wing housed the queen's state apartment, which was a mirror image of the king's on the south side. While Hatfield could also offer state apartments for both king and queen, only Audley End had matching suites, making it the most ambitious Jacobean house built in England. Some decorative plaster ceilings from this apartment survive (see plan on page 48), most notably from the rooms which became in Charles II's time the king's privy chamber (later divided by a spine wall between Lady Braybrooke's sitting room and the Howard sitting room), the king's withdrawing room (in the Neville bedroom) and part of the bedchamber ceiling (in the Howard bedroom), with many of their friezes. The Jacobean chimney pieces are not in their original positions; those which do not reach the friezes probably came from other floors. Although altered and the flights narrowed, the north stair is the second most important one to survive from the Jacobean house.

The later history of the north wing also mirrors that of the south. The north side was Sir John Griffin Griffin's own suite from 1762. The south suite was used by guests until 1826, when it became the private apartment of the 3rd Lord Braybrooke and his wife, and the north suite was used as the guest apartment. Apart from Lady Braybrooke's sitting room, most of the historic contents of these rooms are no longer at Audley End. The furniture and pictures on display here were originally elsewhere in the house.

Lady Braybrooke's Sitting Room

The 3rd Lady Braybrooke (1798–1856) used this as a dressing room and morning room, with comfortable armchairs and late 18th-century French furniture. The wallpaper is a reproduction of a design used throughout the apartment in about 1830. The Braybrookes bought the late 16th-century French oak cupboard on a trip to Antwerp in 1829, while the green tortoiseshell bracket clock belonged to Sir John Griffin Griffin. To the left of the armoire is a 1762 portrait by Thomas Hudson of the Countess of Portsmouth. By 1891, Florence, 5th Lady Braybrooke, had added further layers of rich furnishings, bringing out some of Sir John's furniture whose style had come back into fashion. The density and diversity of furnishings is typical of late 19th-century taste.

Above: Jane Cornwallis, wife of the 3rd Lord Braybrooke, painted by HW Pickersgill
Left: Lady Braybrooke's sitting room, arranged as it was in the late 19th century. She used this room as her dressing room and morning room

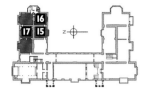

Right: The Red Bed, designed by Paul Saunders in 1765, and its associated furniture, now displayed in the Neville Bedroom

Below: Detail from the portrait of Elizabeth Grey, later Countess of Portsmouth, attributed to Michael Dahl, now hanging in the Neville Dressing Room

Facing page: The Howard state bed, displayed in a mid 18th-century bed alcove. The flower embroideries, in coloured silk and metallic thread, were supplied by J Seneschal, and are appliquéd onto the silk hangings

15 Neville Bedroom and 16 Dressing Room

The furniture now displayed here originally came from Sir John Griffin Griffin's 'red apartment' on the first floor of the south wing, which was the second best in the house. The bed was supplied to Sir John in 1765 by the London upholsterer Paul Saunders; the original mixed silk and wool damask still survives on the inside of the canopy. The lacquer furniture and the mirror have always been in the same room as the bed; the night tables also date from the 1760s. The bedroom retains some of the bolection (relief) moulded panelling installed throughout this wing in the early 18th century.

The dressing room, which dates from Sir John's reinstatement of the ends of the wings in 1786, served as his wife's dressing room. On either side of the portrait of the Countess of Portsmouth are views of Hurstbourne Priors, Hampshire, home of her second husband. The door in the east wall led to a service stair to the ground floor.

17 Howard Suite

The dressing room and bedroom contain furniture from the state bedroom suite created by Sir John Griffin Griffin in 1786 on the first floor of the

south wing, and its early 19th-century successor on the ground floor of the south wing. The richness of the state bed of 1786, by the London firm of Chipchase and Lambert, contrasts with its setting in a mid 18th-century bed alcove. It was commissioned by Sir John following his elevation to the peerage as Lord Howard de Walden in 1784, in anticipation of a royal visit, along with the stool and armchairs and the portrait of Queen Charlotte (a copy of one by Gainsborough). The fabric on the walls is a modern reproduction of the watered blue silk originally used in Lord Howard's state apartment, to match the Chinese silk of the bed. Other pieces of furniture were added to the ensemble later. The daybed in the dressing room was acquired before a visit by the Duke of Gloucester in 1819 (see page 54).

The Howard sitting room has been dressed in the 'country-house' style of the late 19th and early 20th centuries. The pictures, however, were all hanging here in 1871, and mostly relate to the Neville family. The portraits of the Duke of Brunswick and Prince Ferdinand were copied for Sir John, who had served under both princes in the Seven Years War (1756–63).

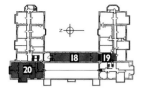

Right: Looking south through the Coal Gallery, with an 1820s coal bin on the right. Opposite is a calorifier, in which water circulating from a distant boiler transferred heat to water for domestic use; the first was installed here in 1867

Below: Carving of a lion from a newel post of the south stair. It might have been added to the Jacobean stair in the early 19th century

Facing page top: A detail of the vine wallpaper dating to the 1830s or 1840s in the nursery suite

SECOND FLOOR

The second floor always provided lodgings for lesser members of the household, both family and servants. On the north landing, the heads of a pair of original Jacobean doors remain visible. These led into lodgings arranged either side of the spine wall of the north wing. Opposite, another larger Jacobean door leads into what was originally a single room (later converted into the nursery suite). It was probably intended as a Jacobean summer great chamber, with only a small fireplace at the far end, but it seems never to have been elaborately finished. By the late 18th century it had been sub-divided into servants' bedrooms, mostly unheated.

The second floors of the north and south wings were originally linked at their eastern ends by another range of rooms above the long gallery. The demolition of the gallery wing in 1752 left the north and south wings disconnected until Sir John Griffin Griffin added a stack of galleries behind the great hall, to link their western ends.

🔢 The Coal Gallery

This gallery was part of Sir John Griffin Griffin's work in the early 1760s, providing a service link between the north and south wings, in parallel to the picture gallery below. It was treated almost as an external space, with the Jacobean windows at the ends retained, the floor tiled and the walls of limewashed brick. Between 1822 and 1824 it was completely refitted by Richard Neville, after opening up the ends to the top landings of the stairs, to bring light to the stair heads. Its purpose remained the same: fitted with walk-in closets (like the surviving one), wood and coal bins and sinks, from which the bedrooms were serviced with linen, coal and hot water, and chamber pots emptied. The sinks, and some Bramah water closets elsewhere, were fed by lead header tanks on the roof at either end, filled by a pump powered by a water wheel, housed in a pump house that still sits beside the river Cam. Sir John was an early adopter of country-house technology, also installing service bells.

'A new crane to draw up coals' (in baskets on a rope) was supplied in 1824; the surviving, lighter, mechanism worked on the same principle. There are traces of an 1820s copper for heating water, probably for baths, but the present one is later. Piped hot water, heated by the calorifier on the opposite wall, was probably introduced in 1867.

🔢 The south landing

The stair is Jacobean, though it has been much rearranged: final changes were made in 1823 to better connect to the Coal Gallery. The huge painting of 1738, by Jan Griffier the younger, shows Billingbear, Berkshire, the ancestral seat of the Nevilles, demolished in 1926. Its companion is hung at the foot of this stair.

20 Nursery

When Richard Neville (later to become the 3rd Lord Braybrooke) and his wife Lady Jane Cornwallis settled at Audley End in 1820, they established a nursery on the top floor of the south wing. But in the spring of 1822, shortly before the birth of Louisa, the third of their eight children, they began to convert this suite of rooms at the western end of the north wing. Partitions were altered and fireplaces inserted initially to create the main nursery, with a sitting room and bedroom on the north side. Uniform redecoration with 'vine' wallpaper of the late 1830s or 1840s (partly surviving, and otherwise reinstated in 2014) indicates that by then the whole set of rooms formed the nursery suite. The schoolroom (not open), formed from the organ gallery of the chapel (see page 14), was off the landing at the end of the Coal Gallery, on a mezzanine floor beneath the nursery.

The Doll's House

The doll's house is original to the nursery and was put together by the children of the 3rd Lord Braybrooke. Some of the furnishings were made by the children themselves.

Watercolours from the first half of the 19th century clearly show the doll's house standing in its present location. The house and its contents mostly date from the 1820s and 1830s and it is remarkable for the completeness of its interior decoration and furnishings.

The doll's house consists of a mix of bought and home-made elements. Bought pieces include the miniature tin furniture and probably also the small circular table with a base of simulated antler horn. Many of the bought pieces are from Germany, including the dolls. The painted wooden dolls are the same type as those played with by Queen Victoria as a child.

The hand-worked carpets, silk and chintz curtains and bed hangings, and embroidered footstools, were all home-made. 1780s curtain material from the Adam Dining Parlour was used to make the green curtains in the doll's house. The vibrant greens, blues, pinks and yellows of the wallpapers are typical of early 19th-century Regency taste; they were probably originally lining papers for boxes and trunks.

Much of this work was presumably done by the 3rd Lord Braybrooke's eight children, who grew up in the nursery suite at Audley End. The disproportionate size of some of the furnishings also suggests the children's role in dressing their doll's house.

Left: The painted wooden German dolls
Below: The three tiers of the doll's house showing bedrooms, drawing room and below-stairs areas

Above: Portrait of governess Mary Dormer from a painting by Mirabel, the 3rd Lord Braybrooke's eldest daughter, probably made in the late 1840s

Right: The nursery looking into the bay window; the door in the side of the bay led to a small pantry

Below: A watercolour painting of the nursery in the late 1830s or 1840s. The doll's house can be seen on the left

The boys (Richard Cornwallis, b.1820; Charles Cornwallis, b.1823; Henry Aldworth, b.1824; Latimer, b.1827; Grey, b.1830) went away to Eton aged 11 or 12, after preparatory schooling at home. But as the girls (Mirabel Jane, b.1821; Louisa Anne, b.1822; Lucy Georgiana, b.1828) grew up, the nursery became their sitting room, with bedrooms around it, charmingly captured in watercolours by Mirabel and Lucy. In 1827, the nursery was staffed by a governess in charge of three nursery maids, supplemented by a wet nurse. The 'amiable, sensible governess' Mary Dormer (1791–1883), in post by 1835, remained a companion to the children into adulthood and a friend in later life.

A B C D E

The Braybrooke Children

'Six [children]... were introduced after dinner: four boys and two girls, all fine, fair, fat children, very honest and true, but rather noisy and not quite in hand, I thought'.
Lord Lyttelton, in a letter to his wife, October 1834

From 1822 the children of the 3rd Lord Braybrooke were brought up in the newly created nursery. Here, the siblings would have played, slept and taken their meals under the supervision of the governess and nursery maids. This was their own little world quite separate from the rest of the house. The girls used the rooms until their late teens, turning the nursery suite into a comfortable living space.

A Richard Cornwallis (1820–61)

From an early age Richard had a great interest in archaeology and natural history. As a child, he visited museums and bought a print of the Coliseum for his rooms at Eton. His interests led him to collect coins and finger rings, fossils and stuffed birds, but in later life he was best known as an archaeologist. At Audley End, he created a museum of antiquities with many Roman and Saxon objects from excavations in the local area and was a Fellow the Society of Antiquaries and became President of the Essex Archaeological Society.

B Mirabel Jane (1821–1900)

An accomplished watercolour artist, Mirabel painted many views of the house and gardens. She never married and lived mostly in London as an adult, where she kept in touch with the governess, Miss Dormer.

C Louisa Anne (1822–89)

An 'aimiable and pleasing' girl, Louisa was also a talented artist, painting a series of views of Audley End. She had a particular interest in botany and became a life member of the Botanical Society of Edinburgh at the age of 16.

D Charles Cornwallis (1823–1902) and Henry Aldworth (1824–54)

The brothers were keen cricketers, with Charles laying out a pitch on the lawn in front of Audley End in 1842. In later life, he embraced the role of country squire, and won prizes at county shows for his cows and sheep. Henry pursued a career in the Grenadier Guards. He served in the Crimean War, but was killed at the Battle of Inkerman, 'having received a bullet wound in the back… [and] a bayonet wound through the body'.

E Latimer (1827–1904), Lucy Georgiana (1828–1919) and Grey (1830–54)

As a boy, Latimer was an able cricketer. He later became rector of Heydon. Described as a 'good but dull man', he held the post of Master of Magdalene College for over 50 years. Lucy enjoyed painting, chess and playing the piano. She married a clergyman and had ten children. Grey, the youngest served in Crimea. He was wounded at the Battle of Balaclava and died of his wounds only six days after his brother Henry was killed at Inkerman.

A This painting of a young man in an officer's undress frock coat, by an unknown artist, may be a portrait of Richard Cornwallis Neville

B Portrait of Mirabel Jane by Eden Upton Eddis, 1851. She is shown looking at a watercolour or pastel, perhaps indicating her love of painting and drawing

C Portrait of Louisa Anne by Eden Upton Eddis, about 1851. The flowers, just visible at the edge of the painting, may refer to her interest in botany

D Double portrait of Charles Cornwallis (left) and Henry Aldworth (right) wearing their Eton school uniforms, painted by an unknown artist about 1836

E Group portrait by an unknown artist of the 3rd Lord Braybrooke's three youngest children: Latimer (right), Lucy (centre) and Grey (left), painted about 1836

THE ADAM ROOMS

In the Jacobean house, the ground floor of the south wing had an apartment on the north (courtyard) side and an open loggia overlooking the privy garden on the south. The loggia was closed in by the 10th Earl of Suffolk in the 1730s, and his successors Lady Portsmouth and Sir John Griffin Griffin retained this arrangement. Sir John employed the fashionable architect Robert Adam in the mid-1760s to create a suite of reception rooms in the height of neoclassical taste, centred on the Great Drawing Room, overlooking what was now the flower garden. Two rooms on the north side, Sir John's writing room and a supper parlour, provided simpler and more intimate accommodation, where Sir John's best paintings were displayed (there were no paintings in the main reception rooms). Leading artists and craftsmen of the day were engaged to execute the designs: plasterwork by Joseph Rose, carving and gilding by William and Robert Adair, drawing room furniture by Gordon and Taitt, who supervised the fitting-up of the rooms, and decorative painting by Biagio Rebecca.

The rooms were largely completed by 1771, but they were not to last. When the 3rd Lord Braybrooke moved the reception rooms back upstairs in the 1820s, in an attempt to restore the Jacobean character of the house, the core of Sir John's apartment was adapted as the state apartment, in place of the rooms directly above. The library across the east end was dismantled and the space divided to form the Red Bedroom suite. A corridor was cut through the northern parlours, which became service rooms. These rooms can now be confusing to understand because in 1961 the Ministry of Works decided to restore the Dining Parlour, Great Drawing Room and Little Drawing Room to their 1770s appearance, recorded in great detail, both by drawings and in an inventory taken on Sir John's death in 1797. Original furniture, where it survives, is complemented by reproduction textiles to give an accurate impression of late 18th-century formal living, although the dismantling of the library removed the culmination of Sir John's sequence. As a result, Audley End today has two sequences of reception rooms in the south wing – one on the ground floor and the other on the first floor – which historically did not coexist.

21 Tapestry Room

By the 1830s, this anteroom had been fitted with landscape tapestries originally supplied to Sir John Griffin Griffin by Paul Saunders of Soho in 1767. They were probably unused until Biagio Rebecca extended them with painted cloths in about 1786 to fit Sir John Griffin Griffin's state dressing room, which was destroyed when the 3rd Lord Braybrooke created the present library in the 1820s.

22 Dining Parlour

Adam resolved the irregular shape of this room by defining a symmetrical central area with columnar screens. Green taberay (silk and linen) curtains serve to disguise the differences between the bays. In the time of Sir John Griffin Griffin, dinner was served with great ceremony in the late afternoon. Tables of various sizes were kept in the ante-room (now called the Tapestry Room) and set up as the occasion demanded. Otherwise, furniture was

Left: The hangings in the Tapestry Room show a pastoral scene with a classical ruin
Below: Biagio Rebecca's painting of the Borghese vase on the chimney board in the dining parlour

Facing page: The Little Drawing Room, decorated by the Roman painter Biagio Rebecca in 1773

Above: The Great Drawing Room, with infinite reflections set up in the opposed pier glasses

arranged around the walls, so that the dining parlour could function as a parade room, showing off the carpet and providing fine views over the gardens. The vase outside the south window reflects the 'four Florence vases on pedestals', listed in the 1797 inventory, as do the two small vases on the chimney piece. The alabaster vases on the pedestals had candle sockets within, to light the room in the winter. The vase theme is completed by Biagio Rebecca's painting of the Borghese vase on the chimney stop, used to cover the grate in the summer.

After the creation of the first-floor dining room in the 1820s, this room eventually became the billiard room, with the screens moved further apart to allow room for the billiard table.

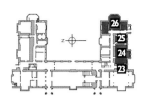

23 Vestibule

This was a simple space through which visitors approached the suite from the south stair. It originally contained only a pair of Adam pedestals to support candelabra, but by 1797 it had become less formal, with an inlaid table and six rush-seated Gothick chairs.

24 Great Drawing Room

Sir John and Lady Griffin Griffin would have received guests here. Despite the lavish use of gilding, achieving grandeur was problematic given the low ceiling. Adam's solution was to manipulate the scale of the room by reducing the dimensions of all its elements to slightly below normal. The pier glasses on opposing walls add a sense of depth through their infinite reflections.

The florid crimson silk damask wall-hangings, curtains and upholstery (a modern reproduction) set the character of the room. The neoclassical ceiling is painted to tone in with the furniture and upholstery; the original 18th-century paintwork survives in the bay. Seat furniture was arranged formally around the walls; as guests arrived, a footman would bring chairs forward for use. To protect the vibrant colours and delicate fabrics, the seat furniture had green and white striped linen case covers and the tables had leather covers; there were even paper and canvas covers for the wall-hangings when the room was not in use. Green painted Venetian blinds were added in 1777. The group of cane chairs in the bay, dating from 1793, reflects a move towards more informal furniture.

25 Little Drawing Room

In the time of Sir John Griffin Griffin, the ladies of the party would have retired to this richly decorated, intimate room while the gentlemen continued talking and drinking in the dining parlour, before the party reunited in the library. The quest for the Antique produced, by October 1764, Adam's design for a room without a chimney piece, focused instead on a sofa niche. The decorative ceiling and wall-painting of 1773 by Rebecca is based on Roman motifs seen in Italy, incorporating grisaille (monochrome) panels based on published illustrations of Roman sculpture. The furniture, supplied by Gordon and Taitt in 1771, was designed to complement the decoration of the room. All but one small 'scrole seat' has survived. The mirror plate cost £73.10s. (about £5,000 today).

26 Red Bedroom Suite

The red bedroom suite, a bedroom flanked by two dressing rooms, remains architecturally as it was created for the 3rd Lord Braybrooke in the reduced shell of Sir John's library. It takes its name from the Red Bed which was moved here in the 1820s from the red apartment on the first floor of the south wing. The bed is now on display in the Neville Bedroom (see page 16). These rooms now contain a collection of views of the house and park, mostly painted by William Tomkins in the 1780s, and elements from the lost library.

Left: Robert Adam, painted in the early 1770s; attributed to George Willison
Below: Robert Adam's design for the Little Drawing Room, October 1764. In the final design, the alcove was made square. The sash windows are shown as they were until modified in the 1820s

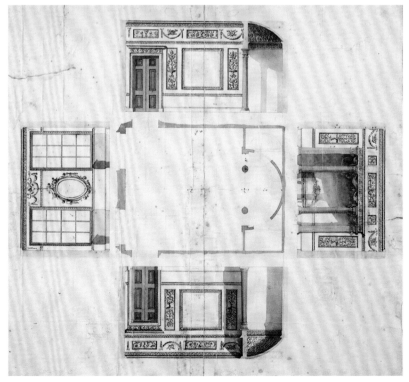

Right: Part of the 4th Lord Braybrooke's bird collection fills the lower gallery

Below: The butler's pantry, with a collection of family silver displayed in the cupboards

Facing page: The kitchen, with late 19th-century equipment fitted into the three original 18th-century stone fireplaces

27 LOWER GALLERY

The lower gallery takes the form of a Jacobean arcaded loggia, which indeed it once was. Originally on the opposite side of the courtyard, it was salvaged by Lady Portsmouth and re-erected here. Sir John Griffin Griffin had it rebuilt again further from the hall, as the base of his stack of communication galleries above. Despite its relationship to the parterre created in the 1830s, it was 'enclosed and taken into the house' by RC Hussey for the 5th Lord Braybrooke in 1863. The reason was primarily to display the overspill of the 4th Lord Braybrooke's collection of mounted birds from the picture gallery above.

The south stair is the richer of the two surviving Jacobean ones. They were altered and embellished by Richard Neville, later 3rd Lord Braybrooke, in 1822–3. Displayed here is a framed engraving of Audley End as a royal palace by Henry Winstanley, clerk of the royal works at the house between 1679 and 1701; and the companion to the 1738 painting by Jan Griffier the younger of Billingbear, Berkshire, hung on the top landing.

SERVICE AREAS
28 Butler's Pantry

This room, built over the wine cellar below, dates from soon after the Countess of Portsmouth's reduction of the house in 1752. It is now displayed as it would have looked in the 19th century. Here delicate glass and silver were washed in the lead-lined sinks to avoid scratches, and silver and knives were cleaned and stored in the cupboards, which now house a collection of family silver. The collection includes items owned by the Countess of Portsmouth, Sir John Griffin Griffin and the lords Braybrooke.

29 Servants' Hall (now the restaurant)

The service rooms have always been concentrated on the north of Audley End. The north side of the north wing of the Jacobean house was a barrel-vaulted cellar, used for storing food and drink; it was largely above ground because of the proximity of the river. About half of this cellar survives in the present restaurant. It was later converted to a kitchen and laundry by the Countess of Portsmouth, or possibly earlier. The blocked openings of the large kitchen fireplaces are still visible. But a kitchen in the house, even in a vaulted space, presented a major fire risk, so Sir John Griffin Griffin built a new kitchen and larders beyond the house, linked to it by a corridor – very similar to the Jacobean arrangements. The remains of the cellar became the servants' hall, with a smaller fireplace to suit its new purpose. The lobby outside became the hub of the service quarters at the foot of the north stair. Service bells were first introduced by Sir John Griffin Griffin, but the existing ones are mostly 19th-century. To the west, formed under his chapel, was the housekeeper's room, still recognizable despite modern alterations.

30 Kitchen, Pastry Larder and Cook's Room

The kitchen is a large space open through two storeys, with a bank of three fireplaces on the east wall, flanked to the north by a block of ancillary spaces, part single- and part two-storey, containing larders and the scullery. In September 1881 the whole building was gutted by a fire, but its separation prevented the fire from spreading to the house. The range for roasting meat, ovens and other fittings date from its reconstruction in 1882. A small pastry larder opens off the opposite corner of the room. All types of flans, pies and biscuits were made here in the Victorian period. The cook's room served as an office and sitting room, where the cook would prepare menus and recipes.

'When my mother [Margaret Cranwell] started work as a kitchen maid, it took her all her money to buy her uniform.'
Margaret Cranwell (remembered by her daughter Marjorie Wellby)

31 Scullery and Dry Larder

Food for the kitchen was prepared in the scullery. Game and poultry were plucked here and pots and pans were washed in the large sinks. Cooked foods were kept in the dry larder, separate from raw food.

32 Meat Safe, Game Larder and Coal Shed

Before refrigeration, game was kept in a special larder out in the service yard and raw meat was kept in the octagonal meat safe. Coal provided essential fuel for the household in Victorian times.

33 Wet Laundry and Dry Laundry

The service buildings were expanded by the 2nd and 3rd lords Braybrooke, the service yard being extended northwards and screened from polite view by the great yew hedge. The most substantial new building was the wet laundry, where clothes were washed. It was added in about 1816 to the back of the earlier, hexagonal laundry of 1786, which became the dry laundry, where clothes were ironed. The fireplaces, containing coppers for boiling clothes and heating water, were largely

Above: Clothes hanging in the dry laundry

Right: A panorama reconstruction drawing of the service buildings, with the north side of the house in the background

1 Game larder
2 Scullery
3 Meat safe
4 Wet laundry
5 Dairy

Facing page top: The dairy, with bowls for cream to settle at the start of the butter-making process. In the 1760s the dairy looked out over the pleasure grounds, and the now-blocked door provided direct access for Lady Griffin

turned around to face into the new building. Service areas always presented an opportunity to reuse materials removed from the main parts of the house, and this was no exception: the hexagonal and square figured limestone blocks used for part of the flooring are typical of what would have been used in the Jacobean period in important spaces such as the great hall.

34 Dairy Maid's Sitting Room, Dairy and Dairy Scullery

The building containing the dairy, like the kitchen, dates from between 1763 and 1765. The dairy maid's sitting room was where the lady of the house could take tea when she came to supervise work in the dairy. In the 18th century, participating in the work of the dairy was a fashionable recreation for ladies. The tiled interior of the dairy, with its shelves supported on miniature Doric columns, goes beyond the merely functional. Equipment used in the dairy was washed in the dairy scullery. The part of the building that is now the shop became a brewhouse, for producing beer.

Running the House

In the late 19th century, Audley End employed nearly 30 servants. The work was often hard and monotonous, with housemaids rising at four or five in the morning.

'In his role as head gardener, my father [James Vert] always dressed smartly, with polished buttons, a watch and chain and a hat. He was responsible for a large team of gardeners.'
James Vert (remembered by his daughter Audley Balfe)

The key service rooms are presented as they might have appeared in about 1882, the kitchen newly restored after the fire. Charles, 5th Lord Braybrooke, had inherited the estate about 20 years earlier, and he and Lady Florence divided their time between Audley End (where during the autumn and winter he could indulge his passion for shooting), various seafront mansions in the late summer and their London house. The couple were supported by nearly 30 servants, 18 of whom lived in, while the remainder, mostly married, lived nearby. Many of them moved with the family from house to house, with a core of about seven permanently at Audley End to keep the house running, headed by the housekeeper.

A strict hierarchy

Audley End had to be kept clean, heated (by coal fires) and lit (by candles and oil lamps), meals prepared and the family and their guests served. Water for washing and bathing had to be provided by hand, the family had to be dressed and their clothes cleaned, and, of course, the servants themselves had to be supported. They operated under a strict hierarchy, with the upper servants dining in the steward's room and the rest in the servants' hall. The butler supervised the men, managed the wine cellar and oversaw the service of meals; footmen did the

Above right: Arthur Freeman, gamekeeper from about 1905 to 1913, probably taken in front of the Cambridge Gate of Audley End
Right: Gardeners in front of the stable block at Audley End, in about 1905. James Vert is seated in the centre in a bowler hat. The garden horse, to the left, is harnessed to a lawn mower

Left: *Group of Braybrooke family servants in the early 20th century. Alice Taylor, the cook, is in the centre* **Below:** *The cookery book of Avis Crocombe, cook at Audley End in the 1880s. The right-hand page has a recipe for ginger beer; the bottom line reads 'copied from Lady B. Book, A. E.'*

serving, as well as answering bells, cleaning boots, and going out in the carriage with the Braybrookes. The housekeeper supervised the female servants, ordered supplies, paid bills and was in charge of the house. Housemaids cleaned, made up fires and did other household tasks, while laundry maids washed and ironed clothes. The cook was assisted by the first kitchen maid, who also prepared the meals for the servants, a second kitchen maid, who prepared ingredients, and a scullery maid, who washed vegetables, plucked birds and washed up. The dairy maid prepared cream and butter from fresh milk from the estate's Jersey herd each day.

A way of life

The work was often hard and monotonous; housemaids rose at four or five in the morning so that fires could be laid and water boiled before the family woke, and scrubbing clothes, washing pots and churning butter by hand was slow and (by modern standards) unpleasant work. Personal servants, such as Lady Braybrooke's lady's maid, tended to have a less arduous life. Emily Justice, who held the post in 1881, was a skilled dressmaker, who looked after her mistress's clothes and jewellery and dressed her hair.

The servants only had one day off a month, tending to isolate them from wider social contact. They would, however, have met the personal servants of guests who came to stay. According to Marjorie Wellby, whose mother Margaret Cranwell

was a kitchen maid at Audley End in the 1920s, and later the cook, the servants ate well. They had reasonable security if they did their jobs well, and could receive tips from departing guests and gifts and bequests from the family. Progress through the hierarchy was possible, normally by moving to another place, and prospects were improved by wide experience. Turnover was therefore quite rapid, with the lower servants at Audley End tending to stay for about two years. Women earned less than men for similar work. In 1881, the cook, Avis Crocombe, earned £50 per year, whereas her male predecessor had earned £120.

Tour of the Gardens and the Landscape of Audley End

THE LANDSCAPE OF AUDLEY END

The site of Walden Abbey, at a crossroads in the Cam valley, provided a first-rate canvas for later landscape gardening. The monastic landscape was essentially functional, with agricultural and other subsidiary buildings to the north-west. A pre-1605 plan (see page 42) suggests that these elements were retained by Thomas, Lord Audley, in his conversion of the monastic buildings in about 1540, adding a formal garden on the south side of the house.

Henry Winstanley's late 17th-century engravings (see pages 42 and 44) show Thomas Howard's Jacobean house as the centrepiece of an extensive formal layout of courts and gardens, organized on an east–west axis, in which the compartments were defined by brick walls. Beyond, to the east, stretching to the edge of Saffron Walden, was a great walled park. This remained the setting of the house as Charles II's palace, and the formality was retained, in increasingly simplified form, through the house's decline in the first half of the 18th century.

Changes in fashion prompted the new owner of Audley End, the Countess of Portsmouth, to soften the landscape, and in the 1760s what remained of the formal gardens was mostly swept away by Sir John Griffin Griffin. 'Capability' Brown began the landscape garden at Audley End, the core of which largely survives today, and Robert Adam designed most of its buildings. Sir John also built up the agricultural estate that supported the house, from the 3,250 acres he inherited as his aunt's share of the Howard estate in 1762, to some 6,000 acres at his death in 1797. The 2nd Lord Braybrooke continued the expansion, buying most of the remainder of the former Howard estate. The core of this remains in the hands of the family today.

Some of the Jacobean formality of the areas around the house was recovered under the 3rd Lord Braybrooke in the 1830s. Lodges were rebuilt in the Jacobean style and, through the 19th century, there was considerable investment in the kitchen garden, as well as the creation of the Pond Garden in the 1860s. As at most country houses, the gardens declined after the First World War, but since the 1980s English Heritage has undertaken major restoration projects.

LION GATE AND LODGE

Lion Gate, dated (but not reliably) 1616, had flanking gateways added in 1768 and was remodelled in 1786, surmounted by a Coade stone Howard lion, with tail outstretched, to commemorate Sir John Griffin Griffin's successful claim to the barony of Howard de Walden. Lion Lodge was rebuilt in 1846, replacing a small classical lodge built by Sir John.

Above: Audley End from near the Temple of Victory on Ring Hill, with Saffron Walden in the distance
Below: The Coade stone Howard lion, added to the Lion Gate in 1786

Facing page: Looking north across the parterre garden towards the fountain

'Capability' Brown and the Landscape of Audley End

Sir John Griffin Griffin commissioned Lancelot 'Capability' Brown to rework the grounds around Audley End. They fell out after Brown apparently gave 'a wrong bend to ye river', contrary to the agreed plan.

Above: *Portrait of 'Capability' Brown by Richard Cosway, c.1770–75*

When Lancelot 'Capability' Brown was commissioned by Sir John Griffin Griffin to lay out the grounds at Audley End in April 1763, he was about 47 years old, at the height of his powers and effectively unrivalled in England as a landscape designer. Born in Northumberland in 1716, he had established himself by the late 1740s as an independent landscape designer and contractor while still working as head gardener at Stowe. He moved to London in 1751, and in 1764 he was appointed as master gardener to George III at Hampton Court, where he lived at Wilderness House until his death in 1783.

Brown's approach was to seek out the 'capabilities' of the place, composing landscapes at once elegant, coherent and functional. At Audley End, his drive between the Lion and Cambridge gates conveniently linked the house and service areas. The drive, along with the public roads, defined and animated a great lawn (or hay meadow) crossed by the artificially widened river Cam. In views from the house this space was artfully outlined by clumps of trees, filtering views of and from the drive. By contrast, looking back, dense planting of trees and shrubs framed views of the house, concealing the domestic offices and the Elysian Garden to the north, and the Mount Garden to the south. According to Brown's contract, the work should have been completed by May 1764, but it was still not finished by the end of the year. Sir John 'was neither satisfied with the delay, nor with the manner in which some of its parts were finishing, nor Mr B willing to do them to my mind, complaining of the expence, which I am persuaded, ran higher than he expected'. The dispute concerned Brown apparently 'giving a wrong bend to ye river', contrary to the agreed plan, which would have involved 'working against the hill'. Brown's contract was terminated, and they were still arguing about the final account in 1768. Sir John's increasingly 'hands-on' approach to work at Audley End was most likely the underlying cause of the rift. Brown's place was taken, from 1773, by the otherwise unknown Joseph Hicks, no doubt working closely under Sir John's supervision.

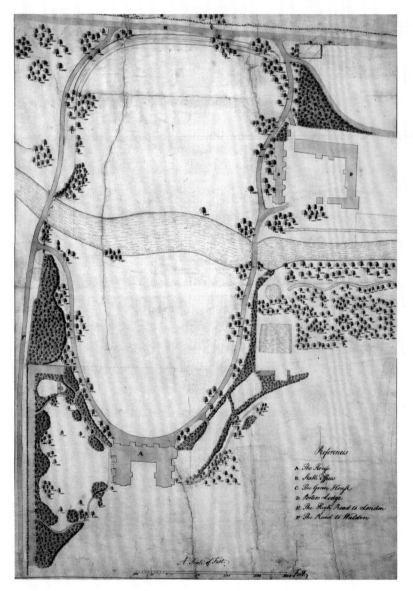

References

A. *The House*
B. *Stable Offices*
C. *The Green House*
D. *Porters Lodge*
E. *The High Road to London*
F. *The Road to Walden*

A Scale of Feet

Left: *Brown's 1762 design for the landscape around the house, much as it was eventually carried out by Sir John Griffin Griffin*

Left: The house from the south-west by Edmund Garvey, 1782, showing the Adam bridge separating two lakes. The upper (right-hand) one is now silted
Below left: The Temple of Victory, on Ring Hill
Below: Urn erected in 1983 in memory of the 108 Polish Special Operations Executive volunteers who trained at Audley End and lost their lives during the Second World War

ADAM BRIDGE AND VIEW UP TO RING HILL

In the late 18th century, the banks of the river Cam were softened and it was widened to form a lake. In addition, the public road from Saffron Walden was made into a feature, carried on Adam's stone bridge of 1763, which was based on a design by the Italian Renaissance architect Palladio. There was a further, larger lake beyond the bridge, which is now silted. Charles, 5th Lord Braybrooke, laid out a cricket pitch on the lawn in front of the house in 1842; later moved to the other side of the river, it remains in use today.

The vista to Ring Hill is framed by planting and closed by Adam's Temple of Victory, built between 1771 and 1773 on the site of a Jacobean belvedere or hunting stand, to celebrate the victory of England and Prussia in the Seven Years War (1756–63). The domed plaster ceiling of the temple has medallions illustrating the glories and consequences of war. (The temple is on private land and is not accessible to the public.) The adjacent wood covers a small Iron Age earthwork hillfort, within which Sir John built a 'menagerie' to keep exotic birds, an aviary later used to raise pheasants for shooting. The London–Cambridge road was sunk into a trench so that passing traffic did not mar the view; sadly it has now been elevated again.

POLISH MEMORIAL AND WARTIME DEFENCES

To the south-west of the house stands the 1983 memorial to the Polish soldiers of the Special Operations Executive, who were based in the house during the Second World War (see page 59). Anti-tank barriers across Stable Bridge (concrete blocks originally joined by a steel hawser) and the small bridge to the north, with a demolition chamber at Tea House bridge (in which explosive charges would have been set to blow the bridge) and another under the Adam bridge, are reminders of the precautions against invasion constructed between 1940 and 1941; others, including pillboxes, can be seen in the vicinity.

Above: The house from the east, looking over the restored parterre

MOUNT GARDEN AND PARTERRE

The large level area to the south of the house was, in the 17th century, the privy or Mount Garden, surrounded by a wall enclosing a raised walk, which overlooked geometric paths between grass plats. The south wall survives, as does part of the west wall, with a military-style bastion (on the bank, just beyond the Polish memorial), marking the line of the front of the outer court of the Jacobean house. The Mount Garden was modified by Brown in the 1760s to form a flower garden outside Sir John's new reception rooms, but much of its formality was later restored.

The changes of the 1820s by the 3rd Lord Braybrooke shifted the emphasis to the east side of the house. In 1832 William Gilpin, a fashionable garden designer, advised on the formal geometric parterre, although the design itself was taken from an 18th-century garden pattern book. It is, nonetheless, a notably early example of the revival of this form of garden, in keeping with the Jacobean revival spirit of the interior. The parterre could be appreciated to good advantage from the first-floor windows of Lord Braybrooke's new reception rooms. It is planted partly with roses and herbaceous flowers, and partly with annuals, as it was originally, in varieties known to have been available in the 1830s. At Christmas the annual beds were planted with bulbs forced in pots in the glasshouses. The water-wheel by the cascade pumped water for the fountain, which was added to the centre of the parterre in 1847.

Maintaining the intricate beds was labour-intensive, and so in the mid-20th century the parterre was grassed over. When English Heritage restored it between 1985 and 1993, the original plan was easily traced by archaeological excavation, because the beds, filled with rich dark topsoil, had been cut deeply into the contrasting subsoil. When the topsoil was removed, the foundations of parts of Walden Abbey, including the east end of the church, and burials in the monks' cemetery, were uncovered at the bottom of the cuts for the beds.

TEMPLE OF CONCORD AND PLACE POND

In the park beyond the ha-ha (a wall sunk into the ground so as not to obstruct the view) stands the Temple of Concord, designed in 1790 by RWE Brettingham to celebrate George III's return to health after his first attack of 'madness'. The roof was removed in the 1960s. Place Pond (by the car park) is the remains of a monastic fishpond, its formal rectangular shape visible on early maps and views (see the plan on page 43); it was softened in the late 18th century.

To the north, in what was the 18th-century deer park (and is now a golf course), stands Lady Portsmouth's Column (not accessible to the public), erected between 1773 and 1774 to commemorate Sir John's benefactor.

ELYSIAN GARDEN

Sir John commissioned Richard Woods to create the Elysian Garden on the banks of the river Cam to the north of the house in 1780, although it was modified in execution by Placido Columbani. The original ambiance is well captured by Tomkins (above), but the green flower-fringed glade surrounded by dark evergreens unfortunately

turned out to be a frost hollow. The garden was largely removed and the area opened into the park in the 1830s. The Palladian (Tea House) bridge, designed by Adam in 1782, at the north end, and Woods's cascade, formed from a mill lade, at the south are all that remain of the garden today, in an informal landscape of trees and shrubs. Beyond, to the west of the river, is the Rose or Pond Garden, made in about 1865–7 by James Pulham and Son, specialists in artificial rockwork ('Pulhamite'), which was fashionable in the Victorian period.

Above: The Tea House or Palladian bridge in the Elysian Garden, by William Tomkins, c.1788
Left: View over Place Pond, looking towards Lady Portsmouth's Column
Below: The Temple of Concord, designed in 1790 by RWE Brettingham

Above: *View of the orchard house which shelters small trees*

Right: *A border in the kitchen garden overlooked by the head gardener's house*

'Wind SE beautiful day. Cleaned up orchard house. Greenhouse and part of stove whitewashed to afford shading to plants inside. Earthed up beans in third vinery which were planted on the 13th.'
William Cresswell, gardener at Audley End, writing in his diary, 27 July 1874

KITCHEN GARDEN

The Pond Garden flanks the kitchen garden, which the Countess of Portsmouth had moved to its present site, out of view of the house, in the 1750s. Sir John added an orangery, designed by John Hobcraft in 1773, which was flanked by glasshouses dividing the original garden. There was a further enclosure with more glasshouses, capable of sustaining exotic fruits such as pineapples. The orangery was succeeded by the present vine house in 1811. An orchard house sheltering small trees in pots in the middle of the garden extended the fruit-growing season; it was originally built in 1856. The west wall of the southern part of the garden was rebuilt in 1802 as a hot wall containing serpentine flues, making it possible to bring fruit forward.

The vine house was restored, and the orchard house reconstructed, in the 1990s, and the garden is now run on traditional lines. The original aim of the garden was to grow fruit and vegetables for the family; produce was sent to the London house when the family was there. By choice of species, manipulation of growing conditions and careful storage, the natural seasons of crops, especially fruits, were extended. A collection of 120 mostly rare varieties of East Anglian apples and other fruit has been assembled and traditional, pre-1900 varieties of plants are grown here today.

Near the entrance is the head gardener's house, rebuilt in 1875 and still occupied by his successor. Most of the garden staff lived out, but two under-gardeners — young men hoping to become head gardeners, who moved frequently to gain experience — lived in the bothy behind the vine house. Off a kitchen/living room were two bedrooms, heated by a pipe loop from the vine house, where in 1874 lived the 'second man', William Cresswell, and the 'third man', James Bedgeford. One of the key sources of information about the garden is William Cresswell's diary, and his bedroom has been dressed as it was in his time. The bothy range also houses the boiler house, packing shed, head gardener's office and tool stores.

STABLE BLOCK

The great outer courtyard of the Jacobean house, crossed by the river, was flanked to the north by service areas, including the brewhouse and the park-keeper's house. The largest and most significant of these subsidiary buildings, the stable block, still stands. Built of brick, with two storeys of small, arched windows and an array of gables and dormers lighting garrets above, it forms an architectural contrast to the Jacobean house. The difference in style reflects its position in the formal hierarchy of the site rather than it being older than the house; the Elizabethan buildings did not extend beyond the river. Henry Winstanley draws it as a stable in the later 17th century, with the tall bay windows (originally gabled) and central door on the north front in place. But these are additions, which relate to an open interior space created by removing the original first floor, blocking many of the lower windows and inserting the two great arched openings in the central cross-wing. The intended first use of most of the building seems to have been essentially domestic, perhaps space without permanent partitions, which could be used to put up the retinue of a royal progress. Conversion to a stable block would then be logical in the context of Thomas Howard, 1st Earl of Suffolk's decision, by about 1610, to add the outer court of lodgings to the main house. To the north of the stable block, there were once ranges of barns defining, on the west and north, a large yard. Only part of the west range now survives (not open to the public), with a reused, probably 15th-century, roof.

The interior of the stable block has been subdivided and refitted several times, the stalls taking on their present form when Lord Howard de Walden was the tenant of Audley End in the early 20th century. The western cross-wing, however, retains some late 18th-century stalls and a game larder. The roof lantern and gable finials were added in 1840 to 1842.

The stable block and the adjacent tackroom now house an exhibition on the estate in the 1880s. On the opposite side of the present stable yard is a brick carriage house of about 1875. This also housed the estate fire engine, supplied by Merryweather and Sons in 1843, which is still on display here.

Left: Loose boxes in the stable, part of the early 20th-century refit by Lord Howard de Walden

Below: The stable block from the west; its domestic scale and red brick form a contrast to the house

History of the House and Gardens

WALDEN ABBEY

The large manor of Walden had been held by the De Mandeville family, earls of Essex, since the Norman Conquest. On it they established a castle and, in 1141, the market from which the town of Saffron Walden developed. Geoffrey de Mandeville founded a Benedictine priory at Brookwalden in about 1139 on land near to the river and the London–Cambridge road, hemmed in by other owners. Although never very rich, it was elevated to the status of an abbey by Richard I in 1190. The Book of the Foundation of Walden Abbey, written in about 1203, gives a fascinating account of the struggle, particularly by the second prior, Reginald, to establish and endow the house. From the 13th to the 15th centuries the De Bohun family, subsequent earls of Essex and also of Hereford, were important patrons, and many were buried in the abbey.

The inner court walls of the Jacobean house were built directly on top of the abbey cloister. The relationship was established by a small archaeological excavation in 1950, against the north wing of the house, which located the cloister walk almost a metre (3ft) below present floor level. The cloister had been reconstructed by Humphrey de Bohun, 6th Earl of Essex, between 1335 and 1361.

The church, largely complete by the middle of the 13th century, was on the north side of the cloister, its sanctuary projecting eastwards beyond the claustral buildings, as seen in the reconstruction drawing above. Excavations in connection with the restoration of the parterre revealed that the east end of the church was rebuilt and extended late in the abbey's life, probably in about 1500. The chapter house and dormitory lay on the east side of the cloister and the refectory on the south side.

SIR THOMAS AUDLEY AND THE CREATION OF AUDLEY END

In common with all religious houses in England, Walden Abbey was dissolved by Henry VIII at the Reformation. The abbey surrendered on 22 March 1538 and five days later the king granted it to Sir Thomas Audley (1488–1544), created Baron Audley of Walden in November 1538. Audley was a shrewd, intelligent lawyer, who was Speaker of

Above: Walden Abbey in about 1500, looking west. The church dominates the north side of the cloister

Left: Portrait of a gentleman said to be Thomas, Lord Audley, by a follower of Adriaen Thomas Key, 1569

Facing page: Audley End from the south-east, looking towards Ring Hill, painted about 1788 by William Tomkins. 'Capability' Brown's park extends to the very walls of the house; note the sailing boat on the lake

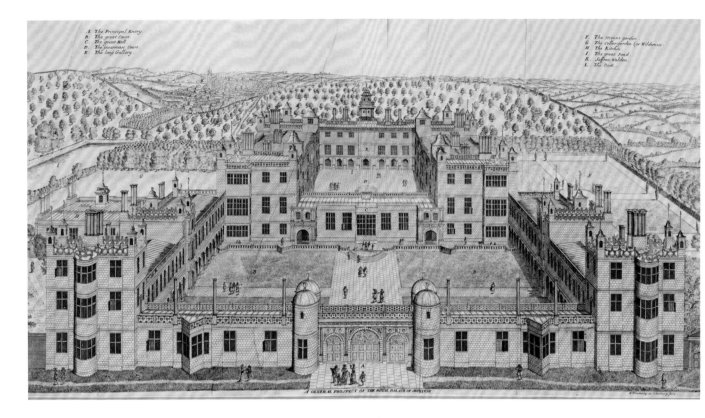

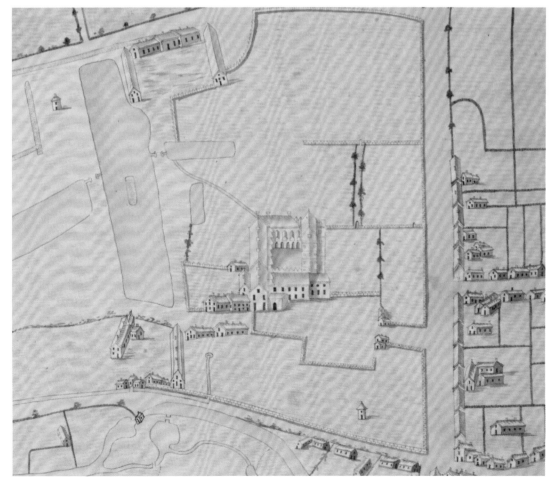

Above: Winstanley's General Prospect of the Royal Palace of Auydlyene, about 1676
Right: A late 18th-century copy of a lost pre-1605 map of Audley End, looking east. The arcade of the east side of the monastic cloister is clear. The courtyard in the top left-hand corner may be farm buildings inherited from the abbey

the House of Commons from 1529 to 1533, in the Reformation Parliament which formalized the break with Rome.

Appointed Lord Chancellor in 1533, he confirmed Henry's divorce, passed the death sentence on Sir Thomas More, and presided at the trial of Anne Boleyn. His loyalty was rewarded. By the time of his death he had transformed Walden Abbey into his 'chiefe and capital mansion house at Walden'. The speed at which this was accomplished makes it clear that, like many of his contemporaries, he did so by adapting the monastic buildings.

The late 18th-century copy of a lost estate map of about 1600 shows the abbey buildings now with domestic windows, but with the east cloister arcade still clearly visible in the courtyard, presumably with an access gallery added above. The north range, which once contained the abbey church, dominates the others, its east end, including the crossing tower, demolished. The entrance porch is in the same place as the north porch of the later Jacobean house, suggesting that

the hall was also in the same location. The immediate setting of outbuildings, fishponds and other waterworks was probably largely inherited from the abbey. Beyond the gate, Audley End village opened onto a wide street, where the abbey had held a market since 1295.

Sir Thomas Audley's fine black marble tomb in Saffron Walden church is wholly in the Franco-Italian Renaissance style. This suggests that, like William Sharrington's surviving conversion of Lacock Abbey in Wiltshire, Sir Thomas's work at Audley End may have included Renaissance elements. The estate descended via his daughter Margaret to Thomas Howard, 4th Duke of Norfolk, executed in 1572 for conspiring with Mary, Queen of Scots. It was his second son, Thomas (1561–1626), who redeemed the family reputation and was knighted by Elizabeth I for his gallantry as commander of a ship in the fleet that defeated the Armada. He was created Baron Howard of Walden in 1597 and a knight of the garter in the following year.

THE JACOBEAN HOUSE

Within two months of James VI of Scotland assuming the English crown as James I in 1603, he had made Thomas Howard Earl of Suffolk and appointed him Lord Chamberlain of the household. In 1614, he became Lord Treasurer, but four years later he was relieved of his office under suspicion of corruption, extortion and bribery. The earl and countess were found guilty, but escaped with a heavy fine and retired in disgrace to Audley End, the main cause of their problems.

Thomas Howard seems to have begun rebuilding Audley End in about 1605, soon after his elevation to the peerage, and the house he completed was the most ambitious of its period in England. Royal 'progresses' had played a major role in Elizabeth I's approach to government, with the court moving between her subjects' houses during the spring and summer each year. As a result, her leading subjects sought to outdo each other in providing houses designed to accommodate the ceremonial life of a monarch, with enough lodgings to house the travelling court.

At Audley End, Howard took this ambition to its ultimate level, by providing symmetrical state apartments for King James I (on the south side) and Queen Anne (on the north side) at first-floor level,

Left: Thomas Howard, 1st earl of Suffolk, who built the present Audley End
***Below:** Detail of Sir Thomas Audley's tomb in Saffron Walden church*

'The rooms are high and hung with beautiful tapestries: the beds amply decorated with golden velvet and silk bed hangings and covers: The gallery, which is very long, was not yet finished: the staircases are built with peculiar comfort: after every five steps there is a landing so that one can rest and does not get out of breath. On the top of the building are beautiful balconies allowing one to walk around and enjoy oneself.'
Account of the visit of Johann Ernst, Duke of Saxe-Weimar to Audley End, September 1613, written by his secretary

Above: Duke Johann Ernst the Younger, *by Michiel Jansz van Miereveldt, 1623*
Right: Henry Winstanley's General Ground Plot of the Royal Palace of Audley End, *showing the landscape in a slightly idealized formality*
Below: *The Jacobean house from the east, when its landscape had matured*

linked by a long gallery. He then went on to add an elaborate courtyard surrounded by lodgings, and an outer forecourt through which the house was approached between double avenues of trees. The river Cam was straightened to cross this at right angles, and orchards and bowling greens were laid out. The Mount Garden was created south of the house, surrounded by a broad, raised walk looking down on geometric parterres, with the more modest cellar garden and wilderness to the north. The result was a palace in all but name.

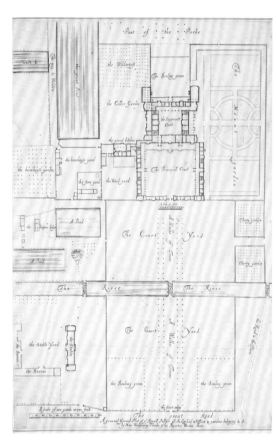

Contemporary sources tell us that the Earl of Northampton 'assisted his nephew, the Earl of Suffolk, by his designing and large contribution to that excellent fabrick, Audley End'. As aristocratic patrons their ideas were developed and the construction overseen by a 'surveyor', who for the first phase of the house was a Flemish mason, Bernard Janssen. Informed by architectural treatises and pattern books mostly published in Italy, France and the Low Countries, such collaboration was the norm before the practice of architecture developed in England, as it already had in Italy and France, as a distinct, learned profession. John Thorpe, a 'surveyor' from a long-established family of Northamptonshire masons, was moving in that direction, and his surviving notebook includes a scheme for the outer court, not quite as executed, and as yet without the porches. The difference between the austere inner court and the highly decorated outer court probably owes much to Suffolk's respective surveyors, as well as Northampton's waning influence (he died in 1614). Within these two extremes of taste, Jacobean patrons employed designers capable of reflecting their current preference.

Left: The west front, with the large bay window onto the great hall between the two entrance porches

Architectural inspiration

Audley End provides a good illustration of how John Thorpe and his contemporaries drew on multiple European sources to create a design unique to its time and place.

The north and south elevations of the demolished outer court were in effect a simplified version of part of the French Mannerist château of Verneuil. This was known to Thorpe from an illustration in

J Androuet du Cerceau's *Les plus excellents bastiments de France* (1576–9). Both buildings had the elevation divided into units of four bays of 'cross' windows, with niches for statues between them (the statues were never installed at Audley End).

The major difference is the form of the loggia: at Audley End this was an arcade carried directly on columns. This was a common motif of Flemish Renaissance buildings, known to

Thorpe at first hand through the Royal Exchange in London. This was built in 1568 for Sir Thomas Gresham by the Antwerp designer Hendryck van Paesschen, who oversaw its construction and supplied many of the components directly from Antwerp.

Right: The outer court of Audley End (top), compared with the château of Verneuil, France (centre) and the courtyard of the Royal Exchange, London (bottom)

Visiting Monarchs

The queen received, among other gifts, a pair of gloves 'perfumed and garnished with embroiderie and goldsmithe's wourke, price 60s.'

Elizabeth I

Elizabeth I (r.1558–1603) visited Thomas Howard, 4th Duke of Norfolk, at the original house at Audley End for a week between August and September 1571. Publicly, he sought her forgiveness for his support of Mary, Queen of Scots, which was granted; privately, however, his disloyalty continued, leading to his arrest and execution in the following year. The corporation of Walden attended and presented Elizabeth with the customary gift, a silver-gilt cup and cover in a case. It was reported that, 'the recorder made an oracion, which ended, the treasorer delivered hys present as foloweth, and afterward, mounted upon his horse, he rode before her majestie with his mace to the hall dore; there the quene extended her hand to the treasorer to kysse, gave hym thanks for hys payns, and so he toke hys leave.'

The reason for the gift, apart from being a reminder of loyalty, was the hope of benefit. When the queen came again to Audley End in July 1578, and received a deputation from the nearby University of Cambridge, they provided even more expensive gifts: a New Testament in Greek 'bound in redde velvitt, and lymmed with gowld, the armes of England sett upon

Above: Elizabeth I in procession with her courtiers, c.1600, after a painting attributed to Robert Peake (c.1592–1667) at Sherborne Castle, Dorset
Right: Portrait of James I by Daniel Mytens (c.1590–c.1647), 1621

each side of the book very fair', and a pair of gloves 'perfumed and garnished with embroiderie and goldsmithe's wourke, price 60s.'. She replied that 'if the universitie would keepe and perform the promise and condicion made in the oracion, she of her parte would accomplish their requests and peticion'. The corporation of Saffron Walden again found themselves obliged to present a silver-gilt cup and cover.

James I

James I (r.1603–25) visited the rebuilt Audley End only twice, in January and July 1614. On the first occasion, he visited Cambridge University, and Thomas Howard, 1st Earl of Suffolk hosted the ensuing festivities at Audley End. It is on this occasion that James is said to have remarked that the house was too great for a king but might suit a Lord Treasurer. In the summer progress the same year, the king arrived at Audley End on 19 July and stayed for two nights near the start of a six-week tour through Northamptonshire to Leicester and Nottingham, before returning to London via Oxfordshire. While at the house, the corporation of Saffron Walden met the king. To prepare for the occasion, they had the 'great mace' regilded, changed the 'oulde Towne-cupp', and bought 1lb 4oz of saffron, a precious spice and dye grown around the town, as a gift for the king.

THE LATER EARLS OF SUFFOLK

By the autumn of 1613 only the gallery interior
and forecourt were still to be completed, so
Audley End was probably finished in about 1614;
and certainly before Thomas Howard's downfall
in 1618. Tapestries on the theme of Hannibal and
Scipio, for example, had been specially woven by
Francis Spiering of Delft between about 1607 and
1611. The Dutch traveller Abram Booth, writing
between 1629 and 1630, soon after Howard's
death in 1626, thought it:

> 'Such a magnificent building and so splendidly
> furnished that it excels all the royal residences
> with the exception of Hampton Court and
> Windsor [its rooms] furnished wonderfully well
> with tapestries and skilful paintings. Amongst
> others there is a magnificent gallery which is
> more than a hundred yards long and fifteen
> wide … gracefully wainscoted throughout …
> But what surpasses all is the garderobe or
> clothes-room, where can be seen so many
> draperies of silk, velvet, satin, gold and silver
> cloth, so exquisitely embroidered and skilfully
> worked, that it is astonishing to find such an
> abundance, of such value and splendour, in
> other than a royal residence.'

Such extravagance had long-term
consequences for the family. When James, the
3rd Earl, inherited in 1640, he had to sell property
to raise about £50,000 to reduce debts. It was
the destruction of many royal palaces under the
Commonwealth that was to be the salvation of

Audley End, and a solution to the Howards'
problems. A year after an inspection in March
1666, Charles II contracted to buy Audley End
for £50,000, of which £20,000 was to remain
on mortgage. In 1668, the Office of Works took
over the burden of maintenance, and the earls,
as keepers of the new palace, retained their
private apartments in the north-west corner of
the outer court.

*Above: Spiering's tapestry
depicting the surrender of
Carthage to Scipio (now in Delft),
made for Audley End*

*Below: Winstanley's view of the
house from the east. The first-floor
long gallery led to the gallery of the
chapel, projecting to the left and
the council chamber, to the right*

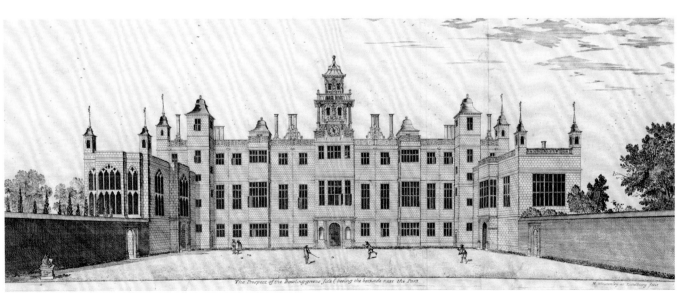

'Many ancient houses of the Crown having been demolished, we have taken a liking to Audley End.'
Charles II, writing in 1666, portrayed above by Sir Peter Lely

CHARLES II AT AUDLEY END

Audley End was built with a symmetrical pair of state apartments. The extent to which visitors were allowed to progress through the sequence of state rooms depended on their rank and standing. By 1666, royal etiquette had developed, and access to the monarch became more restricted. At this date, a true palace would have needed a full sequence of rooms. The layout shown on the plan below of Audley End at this time has been worked out primarily from references to rooms, often listed in what seem to be logical sequences in the Office of Works maintenance accounts. The apartments had a presence chamber, privy chamber, withdrawing chamber, bedchamber, dressing room and closet, with at least one private room or closet off to the side. The state apartments were connected by the long gallery. From this opened a gallery, looking down into the chapel, from which the royal family

and others of high rank would have heard the service. At the north end, the equivalent space was built as a chamber for meetings of the king's council. But Charles II was married to a Catholic queen, Catherine of Braganza, so this space was temporarily fitted up as a Catholic chapel with accommodation for her sacrist, who had charge of the vestments and plate.

Charles's enthusiasm for Audley End was prompted by its proximity to Newmarket races. But he rapidly began to replace the royal lodgings destroyed under the Commonwealth at Newmarket, and after about 1670 neither he nor his successors made much use of Audley End. In the increasingly sophisticated architectural world of the late 17th century, the house looked distinctly old-fashioned and its condition was fast deteriorating. By 1688, when major work ceased, half the roofs had been repaired and releaded.

Audley End in the time of Charles II

When Charles II bought Audley End, the king's and queen's apartments were swapped from their original positions in the Jacobean house, with the king now occupying the north side.

This drawing shows the first-floor plan of Audley End in the time of Charles II. The king's apartments now overlooked the wilderness or cellar garden, on the north side, and the queen the south, overlooking the privy or Mount Garden.

The south side, overlooking the more important garden, was originally designed as the king's side. When James I visited in 1614, the sequence of public rooms in each suite was probably along the garden elevations, with a great chamber (later the presence chamber), antechamber, withdrawing chamber (later privy chamber), bedchamber and closet.

Footprint of current house

Surviving Jacobean ceilings

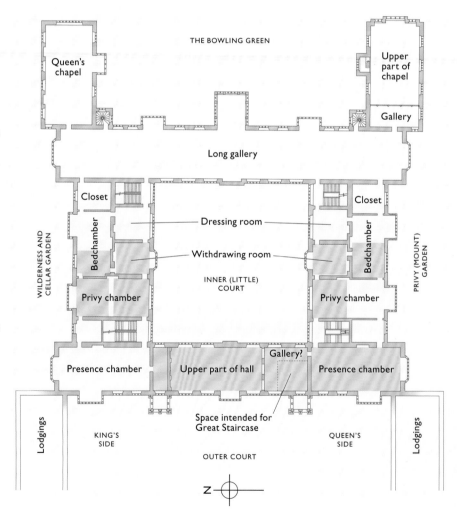

THE HOUSE IN DECLINE

In 1695, Henry Howard, 5th Earl of Suffolk wrote in some distress to Sir Christopher Wren, surveyor of the king's works:

'Those last great windes has soe extramly shattered the chimneys of this house that it is dangerous to walke either in the courtyard or the garden, great stones falling from them daily, and in that part wee lye in wee are in danger every night. There is one great pillar in the cloyster on the right hand mouldered quite away at the foot of it which if not speedily repaired the roomes in probability will tumble downe'.

Decisive action was eventually taken by William III (r.1689–1702) in 1701: the house was returned to trustees on behalf of the heirs of the 3rd Earl, in discharge of the mortgage of £20,000 still remaining.

The next 50 years saw the house drastically reduced in scale, along with incremental modernization. By 1708 Lord Bindon, soon to become 6th Earl, had gained possession of the house and was 'busy to the utmost of his force in new moulding Audley End'. His architect was John Vanbrugh. They demolished the north and south ranges of the outer court and great kitchen, and began to make the interior more comfortable.

In about 1725, his successor Charles, later 9th Earl, reduced the house to little more than the inner courtyard, making a new chapel north of the hall in place of the 17th-century one. His architect was probably Nicholas Dubois, a Huguenot refugee. Plans for a grandiose formal garden were drawn up, but changes were much more modest.

The 10th and last Earl of Suffolk to hold Audley End was Henry, who achieved a degree of solvency by marrying Sarah Inwen, daughter of a rich brewer. The 10th Earl suffered from gout and preferred to live on the ground floor. In order to do so, he enclosed the loggia on the south front.

'The whole lead of the house was very defective, much of the timber was decay'd, and the fabric weake, built after an ill manner, rather gay than substantiall.'
Sir Christopher Wren, on Audley End in 1668

Left: Audley End from the west, c.1710, after the demolition of the lodging ranges flanking the outer court. The outer range was detached from the main house but an underground service tunnel linked the left-hand pavilion to the house

Top: Audley End from the east in the time of Lady Portsmouth in about 1760

Above: Lady Portsmouth in her later years, by Thomas Hudson

Right: Audley End from the south-east, as altered for Lady Portsmouth, showing the ends of the north and south wings reduced to single-storey pavilions. The rear windows of the hall are visible above the re-erected loggia

ELIZABETH, LADY PORTSMOUTH (1691–1762)

The 10th earl died in 1745, childless and intestate, and the house and estate were in divided ownership among the Howard family. The survival of Audley End was due to Elizabeth, Countess of Portsmouth, who in 1751 purchased the house and park from Lord Effingham for £10,000, and added it to her adjacent share of the estate. She too was childless, but her chosen heir was John Griffin Whitwell (1719–97), her sister's eldest son. He was newly married to Anna Maria Shutz, and his aunt decided that he could have no more suitable home than that of his Howard ancestors.

Lady Portsmouth employed the London builders John Phillips and George Shakespear to reduce and remodel the house. The east range containing the long gallery was demolished and the upper floors of the north and south wings reduced in length. The ground floor of the south wing now contained the dining parlour with the other reception rooms beyond, culminating in a library in the retained single-storey pavilion at the end. At first-floor level the saloon, approached by the great stair, had the best bedroom apartment beyond; the remainder of the first floor became three lesser bedroom apartments. The north wing at ground-floor level housed the domestic offices.

All the alterations were undertaken in the Jacobean style, reusing material from the demolished parts, not only out of economy, but as Phillips put it, 'to preserve the line of building, which is certainly the beauty of it, and now appears the same as tho' this was part of the original pile, which your Ladyship gave me express command to observe'. This set a pattern for the future, and indeed the plasterer William Wilton's 1753 work completing the friezes to the truncated first-floor rooms remains the most faithful to the design and spirit of the original. The countess's substantial mahogany furniture, together with her pictures, plate and books, form the basis of the present furnishings.

The avenues in the park had been felled for the value of their timber by the impoverished Howards. In their place the countess introduced informality into the landscape, planting trees in a more 'natural' fashion, both individually and in clumps. She retained the formal approach to Audley End, but moved the kitchen garden to its current location, out of direct sight of the house.

Family Tree

Successive ownership of Audley End is shown in red

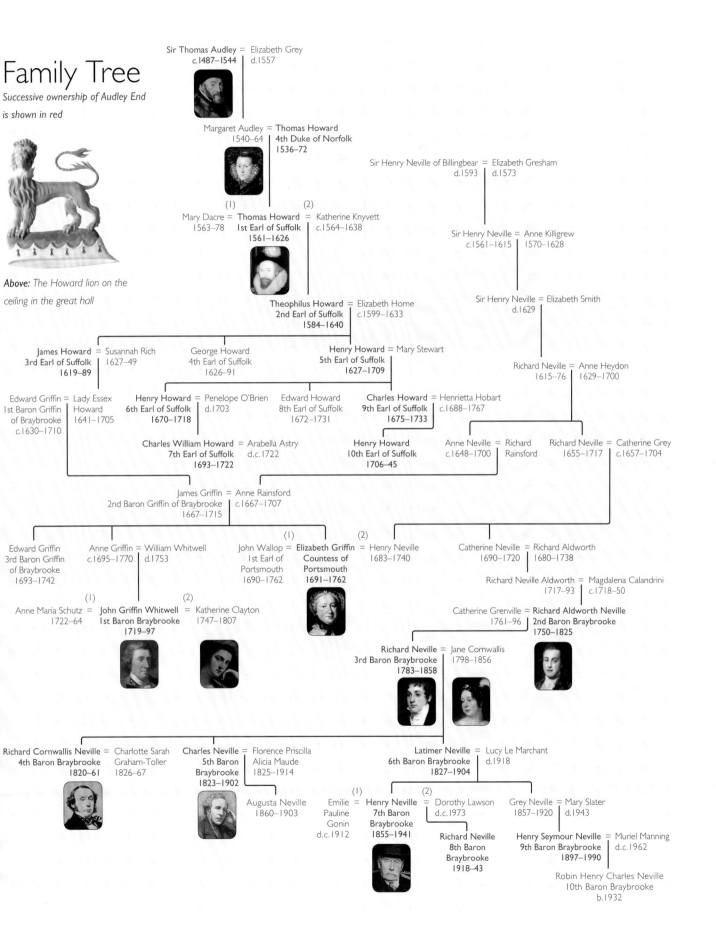

Above: The Howard lion on the ceiling in the great hall

Sir Thomas Audley = Elizabeth Grey
c.1487–1544 | d.1557

Margaret Audley = **Thomas Howard**
1540–64 | **4th Duke of Norfolk**
1536–72

Sir Henry Neville of Billingbear = Elizabeth Gresham
d.1593 | d.1573

(1)
Mary Dacre = **Thomas Howard** = Katherine Knyvett (2)
1563–78 | **1st Earl of Suffolk** | c.1564–1638
1561–1626

Sir Henry Neville = Anne Killigrew
c.1561–1615 | 1570–1628

Theophilus Howard = Elizabeth Home
2nd Earl of Suffolk | c.1599–1633
1584–1640

Sir Henry Neville = Elizabeth Smith
d.1629

James Howard = Susannah Rich
3rd Earl of Suffolk | 1627–49
1619–89

George Howard
4th Earl of Suffolk
1626–91

Henry Howard = Mary Stewart
5th Earl of Suffolk
1627–1709

Richard Neville = Anne Heydon
1615–76 | 1629–1700

Edward Griffin = Lady Essex
1st Baron Griffin | Howard
of Braybrooke | 1641–1705
c.1630–1710

Henry Howard = Penelope O'Brien
6th Earl of Suffolk | d.1703
1670–1718

Edward Howard
8th Earl of Suffolk
1672–1731

Charles Howard = Henrietta Hobart
9th Earl of Suffolk | c.1688–1767
1675–1733

Anne Neville = Richard
c.1648–1700 | Rainsford

Richard Neville = Catherine Grey
1655–1717 | c.1657–1704

Charles William Howard = Arabella Astry
7th Earl of Suffolk | d.c.1722
1693–1722

Henry Howard
10th Earl of Suffolk
1706–45

James Griffin = Anne Rainsford
2nd Baron Griffin of Braybrooke | c.1667–1707
1667–1715

(1)
Edward Griffin
3rd Baron Griffin
of Braybrooke
1693–1742

Anne Griffin = William Whitwell
c.1695–1770 | d.1753

John Wallop = **Elizabeth Griffin** = Henry Neville (2)
1st Earl of | **Countess of** | 1683–1740
Portsmouth | **Portsmouth**
1690–1762 | **1691–1762**

Catherine Neville = Richard Aldworth
1690–1720 | 1680–1738

Richard Neville Aldworth = Magdalena Calandrini
1717–93 | c.1718–50

(1)
Anne Maria Schutz = **John Griffin Whitwell** = Katherine Clayton (2)
1722–64 | **1st Baron Braybrooke** | 1747–1807
1719–97

Catherine Grenville = **Richard Aldworth Neville**
1761–96 | **2nd Baron Braybrooke**
1750–1825

Richard Neville = Jane Cornwallis
3rd Baron Braybrooke | 1798–1856
1783–1858

Richard Cornwallis Neville = Charlotte Sarah
4th Baron Braybrooke | Graham-Toller
1820–61 | 1826–67

Charles Neville = Florence Priscilla
5th Baron | Alicia Maude
Braybrooke | 1825–1914
1823–1902

Latimer Neville = Lucy Le Marchant
6th Baron Braybrooke | d.1918
1827–1904

Augusta Neville
1860–1903

(1)
Emilie = **Henry Neville** = Dorothy Lawson (2)
Pauline | **7th Baron** | d.c.1973
Gonin | **Braybrooke**
d.c.1912 | **1855–1941**

Grey Neville = Mary Slater
1857–1920 | d.1943

Richard Neville
8th Baron
Braybrooke
1918–43

Henry Seymour Neville = Muriel Manning
9th Baron Braybrooke | d.c.1962
1897–1990

Robin Henry Charles Neville
10th Baron Braybrooke
b.1932

Right: Sir John Griffin Griffin, in his general's uniform, by Benjamin West, 1772
Below: Audley End from the south-east, at the end of the 18th century, by William Tomkins; Sir John's best apartment lay behind the Jacobean loggia, infilled in the 1730s

SIR JOHN GRIFFIN GRIFFIN

Sir John had been a distinguished professional soldier, retiring from active service after being wounded at the Battle of Kloster Kampen in 1760 in the Seven Years War. He received the Order of the Bath from George II (r.1727–60), and was elected MP for Andover. In 1762, at the age of 43, he came into his aunt's inheritance, having fulfilled her condition that he change his name and arms to Griffin.

While appreciative of the character and associations of the old house and their underpinning of his ancient lineage, Sir John rapidly sought advice from Robert Adam and 'Capability' Brown, who represented the most sophisticated taste in architecture and landscape gardening. His aunt's reductions to the house had left practical problems, and her interiors seem to have been dull and simply fitted up. Sir John built a stack of galleries behind the hall to replace the long gallery's role of connecting the north and south wings, in the process forming a plan similar to the Jacobean one at Hatfield House. He also built a new detached kitchen on the north side of the house. Adam's greatest achievement was the creation of the new reception rooms on the ground floor of the south wing, but Sir John took an active interest in the detailed design and execution of the work. His second wife, Katherine Clayton, whom he had married in 1766 after the death of Anna Maria, arrived at the house in time to oversee the fitting up of the great apartment, completed in 1771.

Elevation of a Bridge for Sir John Griffin Griffin proposed to be Executed at Audley End.

Left: Robert Adam's 1763
design for the bridge over the
river Cam
Below: Sir John's second wife,
Katherine Clayton of
Harleyford, Buckinghamshire,
by Benjamin West. She
married Sir John in 1765
when she was 18 and he
was 46
Bottom: Watercolour of the
saloon in about 1850

Brown began remodelling the gardens and park, while Adam provided the designs for most of the garden buildings. The remaining formal landscaping was swept away, to be replaced by an English landscape garden, which took full advantage of the possibilities of the topography. Within a couple of years, however, Sir John and Brown quarrelled, and Brown's place was taken by Joseph Hicks. While Sir John employed some of the best designers, artists and craftsmen of the day, from the outset he took a leading role in devising and directing work on the house and landscape. Between 1763 and 1764, for example, he rejected Adam's design for remodelling the upper arcade of the stone screen in the hall. The plasterer Joseph Rose's accounts refer to work being set up 'for Sr John's approbation', leading to completion in its present form.

Elevation to the Peerage

In 1784, Sir John Griffin Griffin achieved a lifelong ambition when George III (r.1760–1820) recognized his claim to the barony of Howard de Walden. He immediately began work on a new state apartment. It was created from what was the best bedroom apartment, opening off the saloon and so forming the culmination of a processional route from the great hall. His aunt's single-storey pavilions on the east front were built back up to their original height, creating dressing rooms at first-floor level, bedrooms above and service stairs and facilities in the projecting bays. The saloon was redecorated as a grand reception room.

Lord Howard was by now an experienced amateur architect and his wife an accomplished decorator. They planned the new work themselves, with structural advice from James

Essex. Most of the work was undertaken by the estate craftsmen under the direction of William Ivory. All this was completed in the summer of 1786, when it was intended that the royal family visit Cambridge University, using Audley End as their base; but all came to nothing when King George III became ill.

Lord and Lady Howard continued improvements in the park, acquiring land from Lord Bristol to complete vistas and augmenting the collections until Lord Howard's death in 1797, 'full of years and earthly honours'. He had been created the 1st Baron Braybrooke in 1788, on the understanding that the title would pass to his chosen heir Richard Neville, a descendant of Lady Portsmouth's first husband, Henry Grey of Billingbear in Berkshire.

Right: Richard Aldworth Neville by Pompeo Batoni, 1773
Below left: The Princess Mary, Duchess of Gloucester and Edinburgh, by William Beechey, c.1818
Below right: Prince William Frederick, Duke of Gloucester and Edinburgh, by William Beechey, c.1820

Facing page bottom left: The great hall reworked by the 3rd Lord Braybrooke, illustrated in Joseph Nash's Mansions of England in the Olden Tyme (1840)

AUDLEY END UNDER THE BRAYBROOKES

Richard Aldworth Neville (1750–1825), 2nd Baron Braybrooke, came to Audley End as a widower with seven children. The house was now in perfect order, and he made only limited changes, waiting, with characteristic diplomacy, until after Lady Howard's death in 1807 to do so. The royal visit for which Lord and Lady Howard had made careful preparation finally came about in 1819, when the Duke of Gloucester, his wife Princess Mary, Duchess of Gloucester, and the duke's sister Princess Sophia stayed for a few days on their way back from Cambridge. The visit was conducted with great splendour: 37 people sat down to dinner in the newly adapted dining parlour.

His eldest son, also Richard (1783–1858), married Lady Jane Cornwallis in the same year, and in 1820 they settled at Audley End, his father retiring to Billingbear. Income from the estate was increased through the enclosure of open fields and common land in the parish of Saffron Walden in 1823, coupled with farm improvements. Neville and his wife made modest changes to the house from 1820 onwards, but on his inheriting the title of 3rd Baron Braybrooke in 1825, they set about alterations almost as extensive as those of Sir John Griffin Griffin; it is substantially their taste that prevails in the house today. Recuperating from illness in 1822, the 3rd Baron, a scholar and antiquarian, as well as a racing enthusiast, had begun to research the history of Audley End, realizing in the process its importance in the history of English architecture. This led to the

A royal visit

'Their Royal Highness's the Duke and Duchess of Gloucester and his sister Princess Sophia Matilda arrived at Audley End about 5 o'clock … . [T]he Royal Party were escorted by a very numerous body of horse men … consisting of the most opulent persons of Walden and the neighbourhood.

'Their Royal Highnesses were received by Lord Braybrooke and his family at the door, and alighted on a crimson carpet spread for the occasion, and proceeded into the Great Hall, a band of music striking up God save the king…

'In a short time, they were taken up the great staircase into the saloon where they staid for some time, until they were shown into their respective apartments on the same floor. The gates of the village were thrown open, and the lawn before the house was crowded by very orderly people, who did not advance beyond the gravel walk, and returned quickly soon … after giving many cheers.'

Account of the visit of the Duke of Gloucester and his wife Princess Mary, Duchess of Gloucester (a daughter of George III), 7 July 1819

publication in 1836 of his *History of Audley End and Saffron Walden*, having in 1823 produced the first edition of Pepys's diaries. Practically, however, his research instilled a desire to restore the Jacobean character of the house, to purge it of Sir John Griffin Griffin's work, from a time, as he saw it when the arts were at a very low ebb'. Sir John's Georgian Gothick chapel came in for particular criticism.

The main change made by the Braybrookes was to move the reception rooms back up to the first floor, with their architect Henry Harrison creating a series of rooms in which surviving Jacobean elements were carefully curated and new work drew on other authentic elements in the house. But their white and gold colour scheme owed much to Sir John, and ultimately pragmatism rather than iconoclasm prevailed. The antiquary Henry Shaw advised on the decoration, but was not above creating confections such as the hall chimney piece. Adam's library had to go, because its ceiling was much higher than the remainder of the great apartment on the ground floor. Had it been retained, its successor on the floor above would have been a mean room approached up steps; but the remainder of the great apartment

was adapted as the new state apartment. Outside, formal parterres replaced the unsuccessful Elysian Garden, lodges were rebuilt on a larger scale to designs by Thomas Rickman and Henry Harrison

Above: Audley End in the time of the Braybrookes, about 1835
Below: Richard Neville, 3rd Lord Braybrooke, by John Hoppner

'Rather a shy man in mixed company, he was wondrous agreeable and flowing too in talk.'
Richard Neville, 3rd Lord Braybrooke, as described by Lord Lyttelton, after a visit to Audley End in 1834

The Natural History Collection

The tableaux of mounted birds and other animals in the cabinets lining the picture gallery and the lower gallery may not be to the tastes of many modern visitors, but they constitute one of the most important collections of their kind to survive in any country house.

The collection was largely formed by the Hon. Richard Neville, 4th Lord Braybrooke, whose passion for natural history seems to have begun at an early age. When he was 12, his parents ordered a cabinet for his fossil collection and some three years later, further glass-fronted cabinets were installed in the picture gallery to house his collection of stuffed birds and animals.

Most of Richard's specimens were British birds shot locally or former pets stuffed and mounted by the Audley End aviary keeper, William Travis, or by professional taxidermists. Others were gifts from friends and relations: the Greater Bird of Paradise originally belonged to William IV, and its skin was passed to Richard by Princess Augusta, the king's sister.

Richard's enthusiasm for collecting continued throughout his life – a mid 1840s inventory lists 99 cases of birds. When Richard succeeded as 4th Lord Braybrooke in 1858 he began to redisplay his collection.

New Jacobean-style cases were installed in the picture gallery and filled chiefly with British and European birds in displays devised by the taxidermist F Butt of Wigmore Street, London. Peat, papier mâché and plaster of Paris were painted and embellished with sand and foliage to replicate natural habitats.

The old cases were refurbished to house foreign birds, including a consignment of over 100 specimens sent flat-packed as skins from Australia. These were installed in the lower gallery after Richard's death by his brother Charles, 5th Lord Braybrooke.

Although unfashionable today, taxidermy was seen as a legitimate aspect of the study of natural history and a wholesome hobby. The galleries at Audley End were viewed as comfortable and instructive spaces to while away a wet afternoon.

collecting trip to the Low Countries in 1828, were abandoned in favour of eclectic interiors, in which their rich collections could be displayed in comfortable and practical settings.

Death in the Crimea

Two of the 3rd Lord Braybrooke's sons died in the Crimean War: Henry Aldworth Neville and Grey Neville. Poignant letters from them to their family at Audley End survive. The 3rd Lord Braybrooke's three surviving sons succeeded as 4th, 5th and 6th barons Braybrooke between 1858 and 1902.

Richard, 4th Lord Braybrooke (1820–61), reinstated the Neville family surname and arms. He was particularly interested in the natural sciences, forming collections of fossils and stuffed birds, as well as becoming a notable archaeologist. Charles, 5th Lord Braybrooke, whose chief interests were agriculture and cricket, undertook major repairs, and enclosed the loggia behind the hall. His wife, Florence, brought surviving Georgian furniture, which was then back in fashion, out of the attics to which Lady Jane had consigned them, to add to the variety of furniture in the principal rooms.

'I cannot tell you, my dear father, now that we are to all appearance on the brink of a severe engagement, how often home recurs to one's thoughts, with the thousand happy remembrances of the time that I have almost entirely spent there.'
Letter from Henry Neville 11 September 1854, Crimea

and cottages were built – evidence of extensive investment in the estate.

One reason for pragmatism, certainly in furnishing the house, was Lord Braybrooke's decision to make Audley End his principal seat, moving the Neville family heirlooms from Billingbear. His wife added her inheritance of the cream of the Cornwallis family possessions, including a complete gallery of ancestral portraits. Initial ideas of collecting antique furniture to fill Jacobean revival interiors, which had led to a

Top left: Adam's Great Drawing Room adapted as the state bedroom, with the state bed (page 16)
Above: *Charles, 5th Lord Braybrooke, 7 June 1890, from the* Illustrated London News
Left: *A grand dinner in the great hall in honour of the marriage of the 4th Lord Braybrooke, 18 March 1852*

'[My husband] had terrible nightmares night after night. Playing billiards with Harry Morrit one evening he stopped dead and said "Did you see what I saw, Harry?" They had both seen a big dog rush in through the wall.'
Margherita Howard de Walden, talking about Audley End in her autobiography, Pages from my Life

AUDLEY END IN THE 20TH CENTURY

Charles was succeeded by his brother the Hon. Revd Latimer Neville, master of Magdalene College, Cambridge, who became 6th Lord Braybrooke in 1902, at the age of 75. He died two years later and his successor Henry Neville, 7th Lord Braybrooke, chose to live at Heydon Rectory and let Audley End to Thomas Ellis, 8th Baron Howard de Walden (1880–1946). Inheriting a fortune aged 19, fiercely intelligent, the only child of a disastrously unhappy marriage, Lord Howard de Walden set about creating a life immersed, as practitioner and patron, in the arts, sport, and science – quite often in medieval or Tudor costume. Audley End had appealed to him romantically as the home of his Howard ancestors, as well as for its proximity to the racing at Newmarket. Under his tenancy in the first decade of the 20th century, the house enjoyed an Edwardian swansong in the great age of country house entertaining, playing host to luminaries such as Guglielmo Marconi and Auguste Rodin. In 1911 Lord Howard de Walden became engaged to Margherita van Raalte, a trained singer. By now convinced that the house was haunted, following their marriage in February 1912 they left Audley End for Chirk Castle in Denbighshire, close to his

Welsh family roots and historical interests, and the 7th Lord Braybrooke returned to Audley End.

Families like the Nevilles, who relied primarily on income from farming estates, had been badly affected by the agricultural depression which set in from the 1870s. Retrenchment came in 1923 with the sale of their other house Billingbear, let from 1841 and left in a poor state of repair after requisition in the First World War. Billingbear was demolished in 1926. Its remaining contents came to Audley End, which Henry and his second wife, Dorothy Lawson, and their young family made their home.

Above right: Henry, 7th Baron Braybrooke with his wife and three children
Right: The great hall in 1907, theatrically dressed in medieval style, the classical screen and stairs almost completely obscured
Below: Lord Howard de Walden by the sculptor Auguste Rodin, made about 1905–6

Audley End's Secret Wartime Past

Between May 1942 and December 1944, Audley End was the headquarters of the Polish Section of the Special Operations Executive.

Soldiers who volunteered to join the Polish underground movement trained here, before being dropped by parachute into their German-occupied home country. Their task was extremely hazardous: of the 316 men and one woman eventually dropped into Poland, 108 died.

Captain Alfons Máckowiak (now known as Alan Mack) was an instructor at Audley End, in charge of fitness, shooting and ammunition storage. An experienced officer in the Polish armed forces, Máckowiak had been taken prisoner by the Russians and then by the Germans but had escaped on both occasions, through his skill, quick wits and sheer luck. He was therefore ideally placed to train Polish recruits at Audley End:

'When I arrived at Audley End I had to report to the colonel [Lt-Col. Terence Roper-Caldbeck] and he told me my duties. All the furniture had been taken out of the house and some of the panelling was covered over. We slept in metal beds inside the house. Even so, I thought it was like a palace – a wonderful place.

'All the training took place in the grounds of Audley End. The day started with a run round the estate, which was a two-mile circuit. I also devised an assault course in the grounds. There was a channel with water in it with trees on either side. Soldiers had to get across this channel using a rope strung from the trees. It was hard and was designed to develop the soldiers' strength. My men told me, "You are a swine for making us do this!" The men practised swimming in the lake. We used one of the garages for basketball and volleyball.

'I also taught silent killing: shooting with different revolvers, rifles and machine guns. The soldiers had to practise firing at moving targets in the dark. I set up six or seven mechanical targets in the grounds, which I controlled electronically. Physically and psychologically, the men had to be very strong.

'We were not afraid. We were just killers – every man wanted to kill Hitler.

'I was involved in preparing the bridges with ammunition. Guns were hidden round the house in hedges and the grounds were surrounded with barbed wire. Luckily, no damage was done to the house or grounds.

'One day, three of us had to stage a hold-up in the local post office as part of our training, and come back with some documents. It had to be done during the day, when the post office was open. One man stood outside and stopped everyone going in, while another stopped people getting out. I jumped up on the counter and shouted, "Hands up! Don't move!" We got back to the unit with the package. People knew that Audley End was a secret place at that time, but they didn't know what was going on there.'

Above: Polish soldier attempting the assault course in the grounds of Audley End in the early 1940s
Below: Captain Alfons Máckowiak (now known as Alan Mack) in his Polish army uniform

On the 7th Lord Braybrooke's death in 1941, Audley End was requisitioned for war use by the Ministry of Works and the furniture was stacked in the state rooms. His younger son, Robert, died on active service in the Second World War soon afterwards, and his elder son, Richard, by then the 8th Lord Braybrooke, and a lieutenant in the Grenadier Guards, was killed in Tunisia in 1943. The house and title passed to his cousin, Henry Seymour Neville.

Before the end of the war the 9th Lord Braybrooke had decided that the house was too big to be a family home, and consulted James Lees-Milne, responsible for the National Trust's country-house scheme, about how to secure its future. Lees-Milne eventually negotiated the purchase of the house and gardens for the nation in 1948 for £30,000; Lord Braybrooke left the pictures and furnishings on loan.

The emphasis under the Ministry of Works and, from 1984, English Heritage, has since been on research, repair and conservation, both to preserve Audley End and make it accessible to the public. In the early 1960s, the Ministry of Works recreated Adam's dining parlour and Great Drawing Room, but in doing so destroyed the state apartment into which they had been converted in the 19th century. This revealed their quality as works of art, but at the expense of the integrity and coherence of the house as a whole. Subsequent restoration has focused on elements such as the kitchen garden, domestic offices and parterre, which were maintained until the house ceased to be a family home in the mid-20th century.

Below: Audley End's west front reflected in the lake